Sensory Writing for Stage and Screen

An Etude-Based Process of Exploration

Sensory Writing for Stage and Screen

An Etude-Based Process of Exploration

MICHAEL WRIGHT

an imprint of
Hackett Publishing Company, Inc.
Indianapolis / Cambridge

A Focus book

Focus an imprint of
Hackett Publishing Company

Copyright © 2015 by Hackett Publishing Company, Inc.

All rights reserved
Printed in the United States of America

18 17 16 15   1 2 3 4 5 6 7

For further information, please address
Hackett Publishing Company, Inc.
P.O. Box 44937
Indianapolis, Indiana 46244-0937

www.hackettpublishing.com

Cover design by Brian Rak
Interior design by Laura Clark
Composition by Aptara, Inc.

Library of Congress Cataloging-in-Publication Data
Wright, Michael, 1945–
 Sensory writing for stage and screen : an etude-based process of exploration / Michael Wright.
   pages cm
 Includes bibliographical references and index.
 ISBN 978-1-58510-725-4 (pbk.)
 1. Playwriting. 2. Motion picture authorship. 3. Drama—Technique. 4. Motion picture plays—Technique. I. Title.
 PN1661.W85 2015
 808.2–dc23
                                                            2015011229

The paper used in this publication meets the minimum requirements of American National Standard for Information Sciences—Permanence of Paper for Printed Library Materials, ANSI Z39.48–1984.

For Hannah and Eli

For Elena Carrillo, Ben Herman, David Mark Cohen, Ellie Finlay and everyone who took time to teach me

All praise to Buddha and His Holiness, the Dalai Lama

CONTENTS

Preface	First Things First	ix
Introduction	Etudes for the Senses	xv
Chapter One	The Olfactory Sense: What Your Nose Knows	1
Chapter Two	Gustatory: The Feast of Living	28
Chapter Three	Auditory: Do You Hear What I Hear?	55
Chapter Four	Touch: It's All Around Us	86
Chapter Five	Vision: The Sky Begins at Our Feet	117
Chapter Six	Visualization: Workshops for Your Senses	148
Coda	Final Thoughts	158

Works Cited	*161*
Index of Etudes in Alphabetical Order	*163*
Produced Works Referenced	*165*

PREFACE

First Things First

"The owls are not what they seem."
  —The Giant to Agent Cooper, in "Twin Peaks"

In the old days, an author might preface a work with the phrase "Dear Reader," and proceed to invite the person into the world of the novel. Permit me the same opening of this book's figurative arms to you:

> Dear Reader, this is not a "how-to" book;
>
> Dear Reader, this is a friendly companion to any text on scriptwriting;
>
> Dear Reader, this is a book in the spirit of playing with writing for the joy of investigating our astonishing inner lives and the primeval instinct to story-tell;
>
> Dear Reader, I am offering an enticement to open up your sensory awareness of the world for the purpose of writing scripts with more depth and texture.

Do you feel welcomed? Good. What you will experience here is a conversation between me and you and your senses. It is a discussion of how our senses work, how we can utilize them to our best benefit for our writing and it's a rolling meditation on the art and craft of scriptwriting.

★ ★ ★

There are many approaches to screenwriting and playwriting. Unfortunately, from my point of view, the typical book on screenwriting is a "how-to" kind of work, focusing on the "laws" (my term) for a successful screenplay. Playwriting texts can be somewhat less formulaic. Even so, trying to match wits, approaches, etc., with major (and let's not forget: *produced*) playwrights can be daunting, if not defeating, for students. "Okay, kids, now go write like Chekov!" Excerpts from well-known plays just seem like commercials for who did it best, once; they're not alive for the reader because they're out of context unless the author wants to provide the entire play, which is what the reader ought to be looking at anyhow. My core advice to all screenwriters and playwrights is: "Read a million scripts, see a million productions."

The downside of how-to books is that some of them might confound you, lock you in, block you up—especially if you are a writer of a unique stripe. Read them, yes, but keep in mind that you can only benefit from knowing the "laws" if you are willing to deviate from them in order to find the path that most satisfies your distinctive inner storyteller. If we only follow the standardized parameters, lockstep, we don't get screenwriters like Charlie Kaufman, Diablo Cody, Richard Linklater, Miranda July, Lars Von Trier, Haifaa al-Mansour, just to name a few in the film world who have challenged and broken past the status quo. The same is true for playwrights like Emily Mann, Heiner Müller, Sarah Kane, Tarell Alvin McCraney, Judith Thompson, or such historically innovative, original stylists as Alfred Jarry, Adrienne Kennedy or Samuel Beckett.

And we also do not get creators who work from entirely different modes, such as filmmaker Mike Leigh, who develops many of his movies by working improvisationally with actors from a bare-bones scenario. Nor do we get theatre makers who create their work in what's known as a "devised" approach—again, building through improvisation with actors and other artists—such as Mabou Mines, The Wooster Group and many more.

So, please do read the books that tell you all about how to write a script and how to emulate those who have achieved success in the past; just don't stop short at so-called proven methods.

What I want more than anything is to help my students serve their own vision, which is the entire point of this book and the others I've written. The worlds of film and theatre are mutable, mercurial. We must keep in mind that these media are as driven by the writers as the writers are driven by marketplace.

Preface

The thing I emphasize to my students is to make sure to see and read as wide a range of theatre and film as possible, particularly from around the globe. "Read a million scripts, see a million productions." It's wonderful to experience a student's reactions to seeing Jean Cocteau's *Beauty and the Beast* when they'd only known the Disney version, or to hear what they thought of *Memento* when all they'd ever known were linear works. I provide them with links to the many sites where scripts are available, encouraging them in particular to read early drafts of screenplays. When a student goes to New York, I encourage them to see work Off- or Off-Off-Broadway as well as the popular works on Broadway, in order to see the range of what's out there. I give them scripts I've gathered in my travels around the globe—plays from the UK, Poland, Germany, Australia, New Zealand, Singapore and Vietnam. I share with them my own experiences of seeing theatre around the globe, witnessing plays that do not adhere to a western sensibility about storytelling.

My perspective on all this comes from my experiences as a self-taught playwright who learned his craft in workshops and in performances, not in a classroom. And as a screenwriter who developed an awareness of the screenwriter's craft by doing script coverage for over a year for MGM/UA, American Playhouse and Triad Artists. I may not have read a million scripts—yet—but in that year alone, I covered around four hundred, plus assorted books, both fiction and nonfiction, and of course, I have read many more since then. In addition, I have not come up through a strictly academic approach to making theatre. The vast majority of what I learned about the possibilities came from working off-campus with an experimental company called The People Playhouse (so-named because our theatre space was in The Puppet Playhouse; we weren't political) during my MFA candidacy at Tulane. The People Playhouse focused on mounting original plays and developing unique stagings of classic works, using techniques from Viola Spolin and Jerzy Grotowski, among others. And in the years since, I have worked in a full range of theatre styles, from the most meticulous efforts to create on-stage realism to highly experimental work.

All this is simply intended to say one thing and one thing only: there are no absolutes when it comes to scriptwriting.

So, yes, read the books. They will provide you with truly helpful ideas. Many will provide you with needed insights into the business side of things, which is vital information. Just keep in mind that not one of them can teach you how to write a script that is absolutely foolproof for the commercial market. This is because there's a secret:

The market is always in flux.

In the film world in particular, things are in a constant state of unpredictability. The space sagas that worked for several years quickly receded into the past when post-apocalyptic, dystopian fables became popular and what will follow the latest boom in 3-D? And when was the last time you saw a western, one of the former stalwarts of Hollywood profitability? No one knows what will be next to hit it big and no one knows whether what is popular this year will generate predictable follow-ups in the coming year. After all, how could one have foreseen the sleeper hits *Juno*, *Napoleon Dynamite* or *Little Miss Sunshine*? Or such fascinatingly conceptual films as *Boyhood* and the Oscar-winning *Birdman*?

In theatre, it's an incessant guessing game as well. So much so that Broadway has become more like "Revival-Way," with very few original works landing productions, or "Son-of-London," with many imports. Those that do make it to the "Great White Way" often experience short runs that don't pay back the investors. It is, at best, a crapshoot, and that's also true for the regional theatres across the United States. One glance at various seasons reveals a simple reality: many of them are playing it safe, doing plays that the audience is already familiar with or at least will recognize. This is just a fact of life in the theatre world, not a criticism. The so-called "economic downturn" of the 2000s put a lot of theatres out of business, so safe is best and hats off to all who survived.

So, then, of course many programs are teaching how-to. It just makes sense and yet does not move the art of theatre forward.

And I'll stick my neck out even further to anger those who insist that there's a method, that we should measure a script as if it's a suit. As the population of America changes toward the date when white people will be the minority, are we seriously insisting on teaching writers from a wide range of cultures that this way or that way is the only way to craft a script?

I hope not.

Before I step off my soapbox, I will suggest two books that are of absolute value to any writer or teacher of writing: *The Writer's*

Preface

Journey by Christopher Vogler and *Backwards and Forwards* by David Ball. Vogler talks about mythic storytelling, as applied from Joseph Campbell's *The Hero's Journey* to screenwriting. Ball's book posits a way of examining plays from a very technical point of view, without asserting that any single mode is correct. Both are open to all manner of storytelling styles. I happen to be of the modest opinion that my books are useful as well.

★ ★ ★

In the process of writing this book, something quite interesting happened: the world decided to help me out with it. Something in a magazine, a story on NPR or even an unrelated Facebook post would suddenly present itself and say: here's another way of looking at what you're trying to say.

Of course, it's me that's doing the noticing, me that's welcoming this kind of input, but it's the fact of really sitting loose to what's coming in through my senses that has made the difference.

This is the absolute heart of sensory work, of writing in an open fashion: being receptive to what is all around us. This world, the people and things in it, are an absolute buffet on which we may feast or nibble as we choose, and available on a 24/7 basis to take in and find inspiring. I can't promise that you'll have the same experience I have had by doing sensory work, by paying close attention to your senses and those of your characters, but I think it's a very likely possibility. In addition, I submit that by doing sensory work through this book and on your own, you will find your writing and approach to it changing over time. Writers tend to think of themselves as output—the person who gets it onto the page—without enough awareness of the input that's assisting their work. Once you open up to all of the sensory stimulation around you and explore it on behalf of your characters, you just might find that you have become a greater conduit for the dazzling abundance that's always out there.

★ ★ ★

One last thing: I have no idea what the quote from "Twin Peaks" means and that's why I used it at the beginning of this Preface. If you look for the quote online you'll find a fairly lengthy discussion by people trying to interpret the statement and not getting very far. The sentence is absolutely delicious in its obscurity, both in the abstract and in the TV series itself.

The heart of the conversation we're having right now is this: what might the quote mean to you? Whatever that might be, that's the writer you are, the creator you are. Your willingness to explore who that is forms the entire *raison d'être* of this book and the others I've written based on opening up your natural intuitive self.

You and I, Dear Reader, are the most phenomenally complex machines we know of on this planet of ours. There are likely things beyond all comprehension—like owls—that far exceed our intricacies. Why then should our work, our creations, fall within limits or codes or modes or any other strictures? Why not test the so-called boundaries to the absolute maximum?

After all, playwriting and screenwriting are also not what they seem.

INTRODUCTION

Etudes for the Senses

"There is no way in which to understand the world without first detecting it through the radar-net of our senses."
—Diane Ackerman, author and naturalist

What makes for a good screenplay or play? In reading hundreds of scripts, while doing coverage in New York and as a university professor teaching scriptwriting, several key things became evident to me:

1. Good scripts utilize a range of sensory elements;
2. Good scripts have an elusive quality that I have come to call texture: a meaningful depth of observation about the characters and a complex interrelationship between plot and structure;
3. Good scripts have a personality of their own, a wholeness that goes beyond story.

The focus of this book is to provide a variety of explorations of the first aspect—sensory elements—in order to help engender the next two.

The explorations are called etudes. Etude is a term I initially used in my book *Playwriting in Process: Thinking and Working Theatrically*, 2nd ed. Etude is a familiar term to those who have studied music or painting. It refers to any exercise designed to assist in developing key techniques for the hand, eye and brain in order to develop a mastery of one's instrument or medium.

The term "etude" comes from the French, literally meaning, "to study." This can apply to the learning process of gathering information, but also to a detailed investigation or analysis. Georges-Pierre Seurat, for instance, did a series of sixty studies—etudes—for his famous painting "A Sunday Afternoon on the Island of La Grande Jatte," in order to explore and understand the relationship between a wide variety of elements planned for the painting. He spent many months on these studies before committing to the final work. In so doing, Seurat developed an individual relationship with each figure in the painting and with each of the surrounding physical components.

The purpose of an etude, as I am using the term, is to expand on a character or plot by writing explorations intended for the script or that fall outside of the script as a way of getting to know the people or story better. It is a way of examining modes of thinking by putting characters into actual scenes with dialogue and actions, rather than by making lists or just jotting notes. When you write a scene in which there is a conflict of some kind, you're working with objectives, obstacles and the thing that really shines a light on character: tactics. How your character goes about solving the problem before them can reveal immense amounts of details about their personality. Using etudes gives you a chance to breathe life into the characters and the story, and think beyond the box.

The relationships Seurat developed helped the painting's texture, as I use the term: each character in his "story" of a quiet afternoon in a public park has the quality of a full existence. Study the painting for a minute and you'll find yourself wondering what they're all thinking and what some of them may be watching since a handful are facing the same direction. Further, you might ask yourself what the weather was like—how warm or cool: one man lounges wearing a sleeveless shirt, another stands wearing a rather formal coat; several people carry umbrellas against the sun. Other questions arise: What does it smell like, what kinds of sounds are there, is anyone picnicking (and what's with the monkey)?

It's also helpful to keep in mind that the painting is nearly six feet by ten feet. Imagine if Seurat had just started in on such a surface without a plan. A screenplay or play is also a huge canvas, so it's well worth exploring the parts of the screenplay or play's world before leaping into the draft.

Scriptwriters often do this work by writing treatments, outlines and beat sheets in order to hammer out the relationships between

Introduction

characters and story elements. A friend described his experiences of co-writing a script as a series of discussions, arguments and compromises that finally led to agreement and thus to the creation of a single notecard to be placed on a display board. The notecard usually represented only a small portion of the story—not even an entire scene. Even so, at the point when the card reached existence it contained enough texture and imagination to be a fully energized building block of the overall work, just as the case with Seurat.

Music students often have whole books of etudes to master and revisit, in order to gain the necessary flexibility and skill to play advanced, complex works. It's about the fingers, of course, but also about generating a memory, both mental and physical, of experience within technical contexts. Musical etudes are also a preparation toward future work on compositions the musician has yet to encounter.

This is of key importance to writers, especially when stepping outside of familiar turf, but true with any new project. The writer often feels as if they have no idea how to get the idea down on the page, as if they've never written anything before. Developing a sufficient backlog of practice through etudes encourages the leap of faith into the work.

Sensory Writing is based on several critical ideas. The key element throughout is that the etudes are focused on an intensive exploration of the senses. For a different type and range of etudes *Playwriting in Process* will be of value to you as well. It offers etudes for developing technique, character, plot, structure and collaborative skills. *Sensory Writing* focuses on etudes for deepening awareness of our nearly infinite range of sense receptors. Etudes from either book will help expand your range of exploration, develop your individual voice and open up the intuitive part of you.

So, why focus on using the senses for our work? Don't we do this anyway—or do we need to examine the possibilities more deeply?

Let's start our response with a bit of insight from Zen teacher and philosopher Alan Watts, from his early work, *The Book: On the Taboo Against Knowing Who You Are*:

> All your five senses are differing forms of one basic sense—something like touch. Seeing is highly sensitive touching. The eyes touch, or feel, light waves and so enable us to touch things out of reach of our hands.

> Similarly, the ears touch sound waves in the air, and the nose tiny particles of dust and gas. But the complex patterns and chains of neurons which constitute these senses are composed of neuron units which are capable of changing between just two states: on or off. To the central brain the individual neuron signals either yes or no—that's all. But, as we know from computers which employ binary arithmetic in which the only figures are 0 and 1, these simple elements can be formed into the most complex and marvelous patterns.[1]

It's not an outrageous assertion, then, to suggest that these complex patterns that occur within us every moment of every day also happen to our characters. This is the point at which you might ask whether this is something you pay sufficient attention to in your work.

Exploration of a given work or character through sensory etudes is a foundation for deepening the material. The etudes may be done for work being planned as well as for work being rewritten, or reapproached—rewriting, polishing and so on. The term foundation implies creating a solid grounding for your work. This has applications for both seasoned and early career writers.

Using sensory etudes as a method of expanding technique and insight can enhance the range of the writer. Many books and teachers advocate writing every day. Quite right—but write what?

If you're not working on a project, the etudes are a way of playing with writing with a simple goal in mind: attempting the etude. The attempt immerses the writer in the task of finding words and approaches to express the ideas generated by the challenge of the etude. You may not have a story going or perhaps the story is being elusive. Rather than not writing, the etudes provide a way of actively engaging you in a process that can open your mind to new perspectives on what you've been stymied by or even provide a brand new story. In the context of this book, the etudes generate a relationship with our own senses and those of our characters.

---

1. Watts, Alan. *The Book: On the Taboo Against Knowing Who You Are*. Accessed 30 May 2014. http://www.beezone.com/alanwatts/taboobook/the_book_chap_1.html

Introduction

The key is to keep writing, exploring, stretching and examining the complexities.

Doing a sequence of sensory etudes can lead to developing ideas or characters you want to engage further. In my screenwriting class at the University of Tulsa, writer S. E. Hinton used the etudes I assigned to explore aspects of a screenplay she wanted to write, for which she had already developed an outline and characters. The university students in the class went with random ideas for each etude; Ms. Hinton applied each exercise to the story and characters of her screenplay. She came to the class with a specific purpose in mind: to use the etudes to develop a deeper sense of the story, people and images for her screenplay. By the time the class was over, she knew what her characters liked to eat, what they might do in an impending disaster and so on.

Working with sensory etudes can keep you open to process in several ways you might not be aware of at this point. For example, the etudes you choose will tell you something about your intuitive nature. The question of why you prefer one type of etude to another at a given time can help you be aware of your instincts. Noticing which sense you tend to favor in your work—or the one you may tend to avoid—will help direct you toward strengthening all of your senses.

For instance, you might prefer auditory stimuli, but do you return habitually to the same kinds of sound/music sources or have you examined other possibilities? I often tell my students that it can be very helpful to listen to a very wide range of music, for example, since we have choices that go back hundreds of years. Focusing on exploration rather than outcome can be very liberating, both in terms of what you seek out sensorily and what you play with in your writing. With the sky as the limit, anything that may have become habitual in your writing can be alleviated. With an actual project you must deliver the script by the deadline, but without a contract or due date looming, explorations can open your mind to avenues of interest and expression that previously may have gone untapped.

Think of etudes as a form of game. Each has a set of givens to play with, but no stated outcome, thus freeing the writer to find their own way through the exercise. The etude concept owes much to the work Viola Spolin did with "Theatre Games," creating exercises that may be used to generate interaction amongst actors in a given company, or be utilized to explore and/or create a script. Spolin's *Improvisation for the Theatre* and *Theatre Games for Rehearsal* are classic sources for anyone working in creating performance material.

One of the things that theatre games utilize is a sort of subtraction of senses: exercises in which a player is blindfolded or where partners are talking over each other without a break to experience auditory overload, etc. Anyone who has ever tried to break a piñata can easily attest to the disorientation created by two senses being hampered at once: the elimination of sight and swinging a stick or bat without knowing where the object of the swing is. This subtractive concept will be found in some of the etudes but certainly you might want to undertake experiments on your own.

We are in a persistent torrent of information, communication, noise, music—distractions of all kinds. The notion of "multitasking" is really a delusion: something has to have precedence over the other things that are being input at the same time. The question, then, is what's in the forefront and how useful are the things in the background? If you're writing while listening to music full blast on headphones or speakers, how much of what's coming through in the music is having an impact on what you're writing? In other words, what are you choosing to be influenced by in your work? What are you adding or subtracting by virtue of your choices?

Utilizing the etudes requires a certain amount of concentration on the specific requirement of the etude. I urge you to give your full focus to each etude and leave the other things out of the equation. This is absolutely crucial with regard to sensory work. As a challenge, go pop in your favorite DVD and watch for a while, and then mute the sound. Now watch the film without the support of dialogue, sound, music, etc. What happens to your perception of the film? Did you notice how your visual awareness became heightened? Now try it the other way: turn away from the screen, restore the sound and just listen without reference to images. It's crucial to eliminate unnecessary "static" and interference from our writing process.

It has been my experience that writers find their own approaches through the etudes. Trust your instincts. What I suggest in each

Introduction

etude is only a platform for digging into your wealth of perceptions and those of your characters.

Remember that the foundation is exploration. The etudes can be used in a dedicated fashion to examine a plot or characters that need to be more fully understood, and thus serve as a tool with a specific purpose. The etudes may also be used to play with your writing and the artist inside you. As previously suggested, they may provide you with games that can sharpen your abilities, but in an oblique fashion.

Games by their nature have two elements: play and rules. Functioning within the rules can keep you from wandering too far afield in your explorations. Conversely, rules can liberate your sense of play because the parameters provide safe territory for your creativity. You could take on the same etude daily for a week or more and achieve different results each time, ranging from minor to extreme variations, depending on the day. In addition, the etudes are mostly done as private work, away from any critical scrutiny or marketplace pressures. The artist needs to take advantage of undisturbed, solitary writing time; it's the only way to keep encouraging our subconscious and unconscious aspects to emerge unbridled.

In pragmatic application, the etudes may be written in different forms: as scenes with dialogue and action or with only dialogue or action. The critical aspect is writing in an active, rather than reflective, voice. Some books on writing will encourage you to make lists, for instance, of character traits. My approach is to have the character engaged in a dialogue or an action sequence.

This gives you the opportunity to develop the character's voice or innate sense of choice in an active fashion. Most of the etudes can be thought of as dilemmas for the character or story—problems to solve. By extension you may see etude work as the same for your writing. As you work through the etudes, you might discover aspects of your writing techniques and interests that need to be opened out more fully. Writers cannot allow themselves to become stuck.

One of the most intriguing aspects of teaching scriptwriting is working with writers from a poetry or prose background. Helping them develop "film- or theatre-think" via etudes is a powerful transition as their minds begin to see the page as a place for storytelling through the cut and image and the mutability of the stage, rather than for direct narrative. Over time they begin to perceive the work as something to be performed with the help of many collaborators, versus the intensely personal single voice relationship of poetry or fiction. As a way of helping, I always encourage my scriptwriting students to sit through all of the final credits on a film or read the program for the play, just to be reminded of the virtual army needed to bring a project from script to screen or stage.

A further aspect of exploration is that etudes are a way of working outside the confines of the script itself. We've all had the experience of feeling blocked on a plot or character, and not knowing how to move forward. The etudes are a means of playing with those elements, but still within the context of an active dramatic life. For example, you may find that developing Character A through memories of a particular eating experience when they were a little kid could reveal aspects of their personality that had not been fully realized.

Doing an etude puts you to work. Rather than sitting slumped over at your desk or in the coffee shop, worrying yourself to pieces, the etudes provide a means of engaging your fingers and mind actively. "Actively" is a crucial concept. It would be tempting to skim through this book, glance at the etudes and do them mentally. But that's jumping over the process. Each time you do an etude by actually creating the scene or scenario, you are actively engaging your mental and sensory faculties; you are writing, and writing dramatically. Thinking is important but engaging the intuition in an active fashion is the purer stuff of the writer's work.

Keep in mind that these explorations are toward scriptwriting and toward your profession. When you do the etudes, keep proper screenwriting or playwriting format in mind throughout your process. Make a concerted effort to refine your writing: generate strong dialogue and vivid action narration or stage directions. Challenge yourself to make any etude you work on a genuinely fine script, even if it's only half a page. Every effort to maintain a professional approach will develop your skills. This is not to say that merely playing with an etude is unacceptable. Certainly you will gain a great deal by scribbling an etude on a napkin. But then take the next step: rewrite, refine, polish—all to build your capabilities. The adage that "writing is 90 percent rewriting" exists for a reason.

Introduction   xxiii

One last, crucial, thought: women and men have different levels of sense perception. It has been established scientifically that women react more immediately and strongly to smell, for instance, and to other aspects of sensory reception. Try comparing notes with various friends from various backgrounds about a given scent or color, just to see where your perceptions and theirs match or differ.

And this brings up an important point. I once encountered a statement that I've used in my teaching ever since. It's a counterpoint to the notion "write what you know," which, while valid in many ways, falls short of what I prefer: "Write what you can own." Meaning: do research, especially first-person, to find out enough about your characters and subject matter to really own the material with verisimilitude.

If you can manage direct experience of anything you wish to write, it's a great way to go, unless the thought of actually climbing a mountain sends you into paroxysms. Failing that, doing research and conducting interviews will carry you far.

It will also benefit you to spend some time actively exploring your own senses, experimenting with them.

Does this also mean if you're male you should try to build your awareness of smell by focusing on it? Or if you're female, try to get a fuller sense of how males perceive sensory input? Yep: that's at least part of what this book is about. Sensory work is about opening up our horizons.

Sensory Writing is a resource for opening (and keeping open) your creative abilities and instincts. The ultimate application of the etudes—and by extension, the craft of scripting—is in your hands: make use of the incredible range of your senses.

And write what you can own.

How to Use This Book

There are several important things that will help you get the most out of this book.

In each chapter you will find etudes that are described for a given sense. Most are followed by a set of variations on that basic exercise, labeled as "Six Degrees . . ." I chose this term in a very conscious way, based on the concept of there being only "six degrees of separation" between everyone on the planet. The variations on any given etude are only a few steps from the basic exercise and exist in symbiosis with the etudes in every chapter. Plus, they can keep on spinning out other etudes. This means that you can (and, I hope, will) seek out and make connections as your intuition dictates. The term is also intended as a reminder that we writers are all only six degrees, or less, from each other, each of us struggling to realize our vision.

At the end of each chapter you will find the term "Fade Out," chosen with much thought as a way of reflecting the two primary performance mediums we're focused on in the book (though I do reference TV shows from time to time, as a reminder that scripting is scripting). The Fade Out coda to each chapter is a way of offering a final variation on the essence of the chapter, usually in the form of a non-writing etude that has to do with directly encountering the world, though there's no pattern per se.

Regardless of what these elements are called, the heart of this book is a buffet for your senses and sensory exploration on behalf of your characters.

The structure of the book is relatively linear, following the senses one by one. Your approach to the book should be as you need, and therefore nonlinear. Using etudes in combinations, both suggested and invented, is highly encouraged, especially in support of a given project or exploration.

The etudes cannot complete your script or figure out the missing plot element, but they can help keep you open to internal and external stimuli, which may in turn provide inspiration and insight into your project.

The key point to this way of working is that there is no set approach to developing a character, plot or structure when writing a screenplay or play. There is no such thing as a standard for how to go about telling your story.

So then, what is your storytelling instinct? If you choose not to follow a formulaic approach, how do you find your way through to the kinds of characters, plots and structures that truly express your vision?

The real answer is based on whether you are open to discovery and surprise in your process. This is where the etudes work best,

Introduction

by taking you on an unplanned journey—a magical mystery tour, if you will.

By doing the etudes you will find that you are much more in touch with your true voice and point of view, and the same for your characters—they will be genuine. The businesses of film and theatre are changing so fast it's almost impossible to predict what's next, but one thing is certain: great, original stories told with excellent technique will always be in demand. This can apply easily to tentpole blockbusters as well as to quietly told stories from regional theatres, and to pieces you've created for YouTube or the like.

Your willingness to explore through your senses is up to you. What's offered here are triggers for opening avenues you might not have readily explored before.

Fade Out: Mindfulness

Before you move on to the next chapter, find a way to take a walk somewhere that's reasonably pleasant. This can be done on the streets of a city or out in the boonies. Give yourself the gift of really noticing what is around you. What do you see, hear, smell, taste and experience in your body as you move about? (For more on this, feel free to jump to Chapter 6 where I have provided etudes based on the recall of physical sensations.)

On another occasion perhaps visit a place that has some past history for you and take that in by working through the senses with open awareness.

For a broader examination of this Fade Out, you might want to read Alexandra Horowitz's wonderful book *On Looking: Eleven Walks with Expert Eyes*. Horowitz states: "Right now, you are missing the vast majority of what is happening around you. You are missing the events unfolding in your body, in the distance, and right in front of you."[2] What a great challenge for us to consider, especially since Horowitz treats us to the process of looking through a variety of eyes, ranging from an artist to a geologist to a dog.

---

2. Horowitz, Alexandra. *On Looking: Eleven Walks with Expert Eyes*. (New York: Scribner, 2013), 1.

A variation on this Fade Out is to take note of times when you typically daydream or space out. Have you ever found yourself at a traffic light with no idea how you got there? Your mind was so busy with something other than driving that you paid no attention to the passage from point A to the red light. If this happens to you on a regular basis, making a much greater effort to be observant will pay big dividends. Start simple: notice the trees or landscaping, or just the condition of the streets as you pass along. Turn off the sound system and give your eyes priority for the drive.

The next step might be to observe the traffic around you. What model is that car in front of you? What year? What sort of person is likely to have bought that particular car? You don't want to have an accident while doing this, so be alert.

We are all so prone to fill our lives with distractions. By focusing on specific tasks and eliminating elements that run counter to a task, we can bring ourselves to a state of mindfulness. Mindfulness is often defined as "knowing what's happening while it's happening." Seems simple on the surface but the reality is that we are frequently so otherwise engaged that our awareness is more of a secondary effect than a state of being fully present in the moment.

The only limit to this kind of mindfulness work is the one you impose: meet the world at every level you can manage. Open up those senses and take it all in; it's quite a feast.

CHAPTER ONE

The Olfactory Sense
What Your Nose Knows

"But *Gladiator* is one of my favourite adventures because I really loved going into the world. I loved creating the world to the degree where you could almost smell it."
—Ridley Scott, director

"I like New York because you're kind of forced to smell everybody else's funk. So it keeps you biologically attached to the world around you."
—Jeffrey Wright, actor

There's no question: it's a fragrant world and the human nose is a super-sensitive instrument for detecting the abundant odors that surround us.

In fact, according to *Scientific American* (March 21, 2014): "Based on humans' ability to discriminate between various close odors, researchers calculate that the average person can distinguish at least a trillion smells."[3] This is impressive to say the least and certainly highly useful for our pursuit of sensory input for our writing.

Whether we realize it or not, we're in constant touch with the smells of the world. Smell is very powerful in our experiences. For this reason, smell and memory are very closely linked.

---

3. Graber, Cynthia. "Human Nose Tallies More Than a Trillion Scents." *Scientific American*. Accessed 4 June 2014. http://www.scientificamerican.com/podcast/episode/human-nose-tallies-more-than-a-trillion-scents/.

Chapter One

The thing is, we receive odors on a constant basis but we may not be paying very much attention to how they form our world or how they could inform the depth of our characters.

Try taking your daily walk or run with a focus on smells. You'll get whiffs of bacon frying or pancakes on a griddle, chicken roasting or a barbecue in progress. Your nose might help you avoid stepping in that pile of dog droppings or getting too close to where a skunk has released its protective spray. Other people might cross your path with their sweat, colognes or perfumes announcing their presence.

If you automatically wrinkled your nose in negative reaction to the idea of smelling someone's sweat or cologne, you've touched base with the essence of this chapter: smell is visceral; it relates to deep feelings that are not linked to our intellects.

Certainly in the animal world, smell is a critical element of survival. Any hunter, human or not, knows not to be where the moving air will carry their scent and cause the potential dinner to bolt.

In the human world, smell is not a survival tool per se, though it does help protect us in various ways. We sniff the milk carton that we fear has been in the refrigerator for too long. We quickly investigate any odd odor in our living space for the source. As Moreland Perkins points out in his book *Sensing the World*, "Knowing what the odor of an object is is knowing what the odor is like. We can know what an odor is like only by smelling it (or by knowing that it resembles an odor we have smelled)."[4]

Smells can be powerful attractors. A loved one might have a particular scent that holds us in thrall, perhaps without even realizing it. Certainly a given odor—cologne, say—can trigger a strong recollection of someone. After my father died, I found myself buying the brand of aftershave he used. I don't use the stuff, but it was a way of connecting, and sometimes I'll pat some on my face just to bring my dad into the room for a bit.

There is a history of using simulated scents in the actual showing of a film, though it rarely worked well enough to justify continued broad development as an aspect of movie going. "Smell-O-Vision" and related technical efforts have had very limited success, for

---

4. Perkins, Moreland. *Sensing the World*. (Indianapolis: Hackett, 1983), 65.

The Olfactory Sense

numerous reasons, though the concept is not an entirely dead issue. (There's a fun Wikipedia article on the subject: http://en.wikipedia.org/wiki/Smell-O-Vision.) An extension of any of the etudes in this chapter would be to imagine your film or play with Smell-O-Vision technology providing exactly the effects you'd hope to have.

The etudes that follow may be utilized in various ways, and certainly not limited to the suggestions provided. They can be employed just for your own personal explorations, to enhance your sensory awareness or to build an element into a character and/or script.

The main thrust of the etudes is to provide a platform for inquiry into your writing. Remember that an etude may be used for playing with possibilities on a script you're planning to develop or it may be utilized as a tool for reexamining one or more aspects of an existing play or screenplay.

Keep in mind that the etudes are intended to be investigations, not solutions. You may find that the etudes that seem to offer an immediate sense of end result might be the ones to avoid in favor of etudes where you have no clue as to how they'll turn out. A willingness to wander into the wilderness is essential, in order to stay open to possibilities. If you approach the etudes as if they are implements for instant answers, you'll get far less satisfying results than if you stay open to the unexpected. Experienced writers know one thing novices will have to learn in order to sustain a career: you cannot beat a scene or character into submission. If the work isn't coming through you naturally, organically, it can often be false, forced or facile. The same is true for the etudes.

A key element to this kind of approach is to compound what you're doing by combining one etude with another. Etudes for smell and taste naturally go together and by intertwining these you may make unexpected discoveries. The key is to trust your instincts and impulses, to suspend judgment and be willing to be surprised.

A final suggestion about etudes is to move through your day with an open awareness of your senses. Whether what you're experiencing is related to a particular sense or exercise, the point is to take note. Most of us carry smart phones that have a memo application in one form or another. This is a perfect tool for recording a momentary thing. It used to be that you would see a writer carrying a journal or keeping a pocket notebook for the purpose of these kinds of immediate jottings. Though people are still very ardent about journaling and keeping notes, it's a great gift to have a memo app available.

★ ★ ★

Before you move forward, here's an observation about smell in a *Smithsonian Magazine* article by Rose Eveleth to pique your interest and perspective:

> What does a flower smell like? In English, we'd probably pause and say something like "it smells like . . . a flower." In English, we describe smells by explaining what they smell like.

The article continues with comparisons between English speakers and those of the Jahai people, hunter-gatherers from Malaysia and Thailand:

> [The Jahai] have words that mean things like "to smell edible," "to smell roasted," "to stink," "to be musty," "to have a urine-like smell," and even "to have a bloody smell which attracts tigers." English speakers struggled to describe the smells they were given and gave answers five times longer than those they used to describe colors.[5]

So, then, how do you describe smells? How do you interact with them? How might your characters? How important are scents to your characters? Are there plots that might evolve out of focus on a particular odor? The etudes that follow provide some explorations for these questions and more.

Key Etude: Smell as Memory

We all experience a sudden déjà vu feeling when a scent encountered in one place suddenly evokes our past. The distinctively smoky odor of lapsang souchong tea can immediately transport me

---

5. Eveleth, Rose. "English Speakers Are Bad at Identifying and Describing Smells." *Smithsonian Magazine*. Accessed 4 June 2014. http://www.smithsonianmag.com/smart-news/english-speakers-are-bad-identifying-and-describing-smells-180949519/.

back to a particular experience in the 1980s in New York City. One whiff and I'm there.

A flashback may be a split-second or longer, but the impact can be profound if we're willing to focus on what happened and where it took us. We may experience odor-related memories several times a day without realizing it, since our minds are busy with so many things besides the immediate environment. Taking a moment to recognize what we've just experienced, or giving ourselves some form of a reminder to return to the experience later on will give us the opportunity to reexamine a given memory and see what's inside it. The memory may be of a moment when a smell dominated an environment, or it may be the link to a series of related events, places and/or people that are a rich tapestry of recall.

We are all familiar with the degree of sensory elements in fiction and poetry. One of the most famous is the seven-volume novel by Marcel Proust, *Remembrance of Things Past*, the writing of which was triggered by smelling and tasting lime-flower tea and a cookie—a madeleine—that evoked a flood of memories in the author and resulted in a novel amounting to nearly 1.5 million words. All that brought about from a shell-shaped confection.

The use of a scent may be especially provocative for the audience as well. I remember an episode of the TV show "M★A★S★H" in which a wounded man is dying. One doctor, Major Charles Winchester, becomes obsessed. He wants to know what the dying man is experiencing. He tries to get the man to talk about what is happening with him but the man is lost in the special world of the body letting go. Finally, when Charles is nearly at his wit's end, the man speaks somewhat coherently, saying, "I smell bread." Winchester is baffled by this but we the audience are not, for the scent of bread baking is powerful—as is any scent that has a special redolence, such as apples and cinnamon stewing or an egg frying. Moreover, the writers of the show used the notion of a scent memory to imply that dying may be simply a feeling of going home; the scent of fresh bread is comforting in the face of the great unknown. It may not have satisfied Charles' by-then overwhelming curiosity, but it certainly assuaged the viewer and actually deepened the compassion the scene provides: we smell what the dying man smelled.

And in all likelihood you smelled the apples or eggs or bread as well, just in reading this page. Powerful stuff, odors.

Stay open to surprises; you may find yourself experiencing something you haven't thought about since it originally happened; your character(s) may do the same. That's gold.

As an exploration of character, the sense of smell as memory can be very powerful. You can approach this etude in a variety of ways.

First, if you are simply exploring possibilities for characters, perhaps without even having a specific plot delineated yet, you can create key aspects of a character's personality through smell as memory. Make a list of smells that strike you as particularly evocative. Don't shy away from unpleasant odors; list smells that you love, that you hate and that you are aware of without a particular feeling toward them. Consider the character you want to explore, and see if any of the smells on your list might hit that character in a visceral way. If nothing lands, revisit your list until something emerges that has a strong effect on the character, if only for a moment.

Give the character the opportunity to describe and/or reencounter the memory in a dialogue with another character. This may also be done as a monologue, of course, though I urge you to focus on writing scenes because of the innately dynamic nature of dramatic confrontation. If you choose to create a monologue, keep in mind that it must have stakes for the character, something at great risk, just as the dialogue must, and not be an "I remember" speech that has little to no dramatic value. The purpose of any etude is to help you find or deepen a character's voice and/or an aspect of the story. In particular, your ambition is to tap into that character's world at a vulnerable, at-risk place.

You may also wish to place the character in an action sequence without dialogue, in which the smell as memory causes them to behave in a certain way, such as going into avoidance mode or becoming exceptionally aggressive when they encounter a smell that overstimulates them in some fashion. This can provide you with a much greater sense of visual storytelling. When you're writing for the screen, try to refine any work you're doing by eliminating as much dialogue as you can in favor of showing the story.

Remember that the character may not know what is affecting them or even that they're being affected. The point is to place them in situations where something is creating a reaction.

Stay open as well to the possibility that the character may have a variety of reactions to a given smell, depending on the circumstances.

Smells that are associated with a sequence of events or a relationship may provoke a pleasant memory one day and something quite different the next. When working with memory keep in mind that a) memory is unreliable, so nothing is 100 percent true, which reminds us that memory is mutable; b) your character's reaction to a given memory is entirely subjective; and c) memory always involves events that may or may not be fully reconciled for the character. If your character encounters a scent that takes them into a place where the experiences have not reached complete closure, it might be quite painful for them. For the writer, this can be rich stuff, since a character in crisis is the stuff of drama.

Six Degrees . . .

If you are exploring a character that you've already given some in-depth thought to, but have yet to find a plot, smell as memory can open some doors for plot possibilities.

For example, a plot might evolve from the way in which a smell suddenly evokes a forgotten place or person. Whether the forgetting is intentional or not is another element you can add to the mix. A recollection coming up on someone totally unexpectedly can certainly be a very powerful stimulus. Conversely, what a character has intentionally buried can be quite unpredictable when finally released. These kinds of reactions can be high drama or comedy. If you are willing to work with your own sense reactions to smell and explore the full range of memories being evoked, you will be emboldened to take your characters to their highest degree of risk.

To work on variations for this etude—or any in the entire book—consider what you know about your character's history. Questions can help. Consider what you want to know about the character's background. Stay open to your curiosities and pursue them to their farthest ends. In this kind of process, everything is within the worlds you are exploring; so if you want to speculate about a character's hygiene or sexual tastes or anything else that may be profoundly personal, do not confine yourself to polite querying. Take every risk on their—and your—behalf in order to open up the world.

To assist this, focus your process. Why were you attracted to the character in the first place? What thing in their history is the most complex for them to deal with? How aware are they of their past or of their feelings? What is the one thing they are deeply ashamed or proud of that they might never reveal to anyone else? In this kind of approach you are an investigator with no limits as to what you can speculate about in a character. A willingness to pursue your deepest curiosity unchecked is the stuff of making art.

As you explore this, keep in mind that the story you'll want to write may be in the past when you assumed it would be in the present. Perhaps the scent memory must be shown in the time of occurrence—in the past—rather than in reflection from the present. Give your story room to identify its own nature.

If you are working with a character you know very well, who is already in a screenplay or play, this etude is ideal for fleshing out your character. Doing explorations of your character through smell as memory may not have any impact on your script's plot, but you will be more in touch with their worldview and background, which can help to deepen their personality.

In my experience of reading plays and screenplays, I have found too many scripts with characters written in a shallow fashion, where it's clear that the character only represents a "quality" to the scriptwriter (he is proud, she is resolute, he is fearful, she is tender), rather than a fully dimensional human being. Because smells often arrive unannounced and can provoke an unexpected memory in us, your character may experience the same thing. This can open interesting layers in them for you: the proud character may be deeply invested in hiding a past that is evoked by the sudden arrival of a particular scent. In discovering this sort of aspect about your character you enable yourself to write more genuine, three-dimensional people.

For this version of the etude you can begin from a set of questions, just riffing as you build toward smell as memory for the character. What is their favorite smell? What is their least favorite? What smell dominates their home environment on a given day? What smell(s) do they associate with their work place and their travel to work? Moving to the memory, then, you can ask the following: What smell evokes a sense of previous homes or childhood or love or guilt or [fill in the blank] for the character? What smell would be the most unpleasant surprise? What would be the most pleasant? What odor might be the one that unlocks an aspect about the character you haven't considered? What would be the most surprising?

Once you've played with these questions, determine which is the most intriguing and enlivening for your character. Explore the question as a dialogue or an action sequence, so that you're placing your character in a dramatic context. The etudes may have nothing to do with your plot whatsoever, but they will teach you much about the nature of the character and you may find new energy for working on that character or the entire project. When you return to your screenplay, you'll know the character(s) better, and may find that their actions and reactions can be improved through newly informed rewriting.

This aspect of the key etude is almost like introducing actors to the material and building on their personalities to enrich the script. In fact, you could add that step as another way of approaching this exercise. Invite actors to read your material and once they're familiar with the characters, ask them to help explore the personalities via sensory work. This could also be very tricky, in that all artists tend to insert their own personalities into work they undertake. Be sure to know your actors well and maintain an open sense about your characters, as things may change quite a bit. Sense memory is powerful for everyone.

There's no limit to the ways in which you can use this key etude. Smell as a form of recall is a constant presence in our lives and can be for the lives of your characters. What you learn for your characters may never appear in the script itself but can serve as a reminder that the characters had lives before the time of the story and will (except for those you kill off) have lives afterwards. The more we are aware that the time of a script is when whatever had been normal has suddenly ceased to be, the more satisfying our work can be—to ourselves and our audiences. In keeping focus on the plot as one portion of an existence, we pay tribute to our audiences by creating characters who have the same longings and conflicts the audience members experience. Utilizing this, we can be more effective in selecting the critical elements of character, plot and structure.

Much Nose Etude

For this etude, whether for a character you wish to develop or an existing one, play with the notion that your character has an exceptional sense of smell. This can go all the way to the point of being superhuman, if it suits the genre and character. And even if it doesn't, it might be a great way of breaking free of your assumptions about the character. Any kind of extreme exploration can do this for you with all of the etudes.

Place the character in various circumstances where the sense of smell overwhelms them. The obvious choice is comedy but there's no reason why an exploration can't exceed the most immediate impulse. You may find that doing an etude that goes against your most natural style and instinct can be very liberating at times. One of the assignments in my upper-level screenwriting class is: "Write in a genre that you absolutely fear or hate or know little about." My students find this taxing but ultimately rewarding.

As one example of scent being devastating, suppose that the heightened sense of smell has driven your character into a housebound circumstance, surrounded by all manner of technology designed to eliminate any kinds of odors. What will happen if some great problem arises that threatens to force the character out into the world? Or something simple, like the power going out? How will they find a way to cope?

This brings us to a brief consideration of the nature of tactics. One of the most important awarenesses writers must have is of the tactics a given character will employ to achieve their goal(s). Any given objective will meet with obstacles—the stronger the obstacle (both internal and external) the better. Sometimes a given moment in a script falters because the tactics the writer chooses are either too obvious, too easy to achieve or completely unbelievable given what we know about the character up to that moment. The more effort you're willing to put into considering the fullest range of tactics for a given character's dilemma, the better. This etude is a good start for that thought process. It offers the possibility of myriad choices, easily ranging from the totally absurd to the most profoundly human ways of coping.

In my class I do a quick exercise with students: "You're trapped in a closet, how do you get out?" The easy answers usually include knocking the door down, calling for help, etc. The best answer ever? "I would turn to smoke and go through the keyhole." That response was certainly a most intriguing and unique sense of tactic. It certainly alerted me to the serendipitous nature of the student and I've remembered their response for decades.

Six Degrees...

One simple variation on the etude would be for the heightened sense of smell to be isolated to a particular scent or odor. Certain perfumes, for example, can drive me out of a room in a fit of sneezing. Others can send me into a state of reverie.

Consider the multitude of possibilities such a relatively narrow stimulus might provoke. What if your character's reactions are extremely different to a single scent depending on the day or context—or even minute by minute? What if their heightened sense of smell only occurs once a day, but at random? You can see how easily this etude can be expanded in as many ways as you wish.

Having a heightened ability could also be an asset for story. The novel, and subsequent film, *Perfume: The Story of a Murderer* is a perfect example of using this as both a character aspect as well as the foundation for a plot.

Another take would be if the heightened sense of smell triggers an extreme reaction in another sense of the character, or diminishes it. What if the character's hearing is suddenly super-sensitive, or goes away completely because of an unexpectedly heightened reaction to an odor?

This etude can take you into some silly places and possibly into some dark ones. Trust your instinct, and keep in mind that each choice opens up a door to another choice. The linkage between these choices may reveal plot aspects to you as well as character facets. Remember: etudes are for exploration, not results.

No Nose Etude

This etude invites you to explore what might befall a character who has absolutely no sense of smell. As with the previous etude, your first choice might be comedy. Seems kind of funny that someone can't smell stuff, but if we look at the reality of this dysfunction, that direction may lose its appeal. The technical term for the medical condition is anosmia, an incapacity to perceive odor or the lack of functioning olfactory glands. Anosmia may be temporary, but traumatic anosmia can be permanent. Anosmia is due to an inflammation or blockage of nasal passages or severe trauma to the brain through an accident to the head.

The comedy side can certainly be explored, while keeping the options open for much more serious possibilities. It all depends on your sense of humor and certainly on the context of your character's circumstances. Even if comedy seems to be the only choice, keep in mind that there are some types of comedy that might stretch your concept beyond the most immediate choice. Farce, or physical comedy, opens up one avenue, while romantic comedy takes us down another, and satire/black comedy is a different road altogether. And, if you keep yourself open to the possibilities, the inability to smell could easily lead to all manner of difficult, if not tragic, results. Any lack of a vital sense opens people up to great risk.

For example, the way that natural gas "smells" is entirely created so that anyone can detect its presence and report the leak. Natural gas is actually colorless and odorless, so a chemical called mercaptan is added, which makes natural gas smell like sulfur or rotten eggs (a smart choice, since we notice this stink very quickly). The reason for this is because many people died years back from their gas lamps before mercaptan was introduced into the mix. Some would forget to turn off the lamp, blowing out the flame instead as if it was a candle and asphyxiate from breathing the gas. Others would go to relight a lamp that had been blown out and the gas buildup would explode. The incorporated smell was clearly protecting the people from themselves.

What if your character is somewhere where the gas has been left on and they can't smell it? What if we know that a bad guy wears a distinctive cologne (perhaps offensively distinct) but the main character has no scent awareness? What if a woman is constantly pursued by men because she gives off a natural scent that attracts them unconsciously, but the man of her dreams has no sense of smell? Go as far as you can with these possibilities, just to see how far to push the envelope in this particular sense.

Six Degrees . . .

With both of these etudes—Much Nose and No Nose—consider the possibilities for plot and structure as well as character when you explore. We've had several great examples of disrupted or distorted visual sense as an element of story and/or structure in films—*Memento* and *Eternal Sunshine of the Spotless Mind*, among others—and plays, going back to *Oedipus Rex* and *King Lear* to the 2012 Pulitzer Prize–winning play, *Water by the Spoonful* by Quiara Alegría Hudes, in which characters only "see" each other as chat lines—so why not a disrupted sense of smell? This may seem a bit of a reach, but everything depends on your inventiveness as a scriptwriter.

It might help to review some of your favorite films or plays and see where and how the sense of smell is evoked in those. It might not be on the surface, but part of the background or a secondary affect. In the first *The Godfather* film, Richard Castellano's character, Clemenza, teaches Al Pacino's character how to make a pasta tomato sauce. It's a simple task, yet one that we can smell easily as he describes each added element, especially garlic frying. It takes on even greater significance when we realize it's associated with "going to the mattresses," i.e., gang warfare, amongst various mafia factions. Later, when the war has actually broken out, we are shown the men sleeping on bare mattresses, sweating in the heat, and an entirely other sense of odor creeps in. More recently, consider references to odors in *Juno* or what the character Napoleon Dynamite smells like from carrying around Tater Tots in his pocket all day.

Sometimes smell is almost a character, even if it's not discussed per se. Imagine, for instance, the range of smells in the famous scene from the fourth episode ("A New Hope," 1977) of *Star Wars* when the main characters fall into the space station's waste disposal area. The title *Scent of a Woman* does much to provoke our imaginations even before seeing the film, and reminds us that one missing sense can heighten another. Tina Howe's lovely play The *Art of Dining* is rife with smells because there is actual cooking onstage. Shakespeare's plays are full of smell references: "A rose by any other name would smell as sweet," from *Romeo and Juliet*, for example. A fun exercise would be to make a list of instances where smell is evoked in scripts you admire; it may surprise you.

Smell Addiction Etude

What if your main character is helplessly dependent on a particular scent? What if the scent is elusive or insanely expensive or only obtainable for one day a year or one second of that day?

What tactics would your character employ to get to that scent? What methods would they be willing to use to "kick" the addiction? What is the source of the addiction? Is it psychological or physiological? How long have they been addicted? How does this addiction affect their relationships, homelife or work? If they could suddenly have an endless supply of the scent they crave, what would their life be like? Is it possible to overdose on a scent? Ask men as they skirt what I call "perfume snipers" in a department store. Ask someone trapped in a taxi with a driver who has hung multiple heavily scented "air fresheners" from his rearview mirror. What helps his taxi smell good to him might give you a blinding headache.

One important process for our work is to utilize the tool of "what-if," especially in regard to outcomes. If we avoid falling into easy solutions our work will be that much stronger. Dreaming through what-if from any starting point and allowing the what-if to keep on complicating is a great way to avoid being simplistic.

For instance, what if your character's smell addiction literally changes their physical reality? You have probably seen cartoons where a character floats through the air on a scent of some kind. Perhaps we humans don't do this, exactly, but a really potent smell can pull us toward it as if our feet could leave the ground. What if this happened to your character?

The more we look at the things our characters desire (even if, as their creators, we know full well they'll never get them), the better we'll understand their natures and tendencies. If you take any character you love from a given film or play and trace what they hope for versus what they actually get, you'll discover intriguing things about that character and their journey through the story. Insights will emerge, based on such factors as what they are willing to do to obtain their desires or what they are willing to compromise on, and why they desire that particular outcome.

What we're like as people is as much a function of what we desire as it is a function of what we do. When we enter the arena of addiction, the stakes are instantly raised many notches. Hope becomes partnered by despair as the person is ceaselessly driven by their addiction.

To do this with your own characters is to encounter their humanity square on, if for no other reason than how people are in real life, constantly living toward the future, despite the irony that, as John Lennon reminded us, "Life is what happens to you while you're busy making other plans."

In a way, addiction is similar. We crave something and find some means of satisfying the craving, whether it's for the thing itself (go have that chocolate), or for what the thing is often a substitute (scientists tell us that the chemicals in chocolate stimulate reactions in us that are similar to the feelings provoked when in love).

Six Degrees . . .

Addictions in general are well worth exploring. An addiction is the extreme condition of habit. In general, we don't think much about our habits, unless or until someone says we need to curtail them. When smoking was banned in various states, people went crazy. They didn't want to give up their way of existing at first, but then some people were able to quit because the situation forced them to examine their habit and ask whether they absolutely needed to continue it. Others discovered that it was actually great to be able to leave their desk and go outside for ten minutes now and then, which put an entirely different slant on their habit, forming a sort of double addiction, both to nicotine and to breaks. In the present time, the ability to get nicotine from vapor e-cigarettes has created an entirely new subset of addictions. The sudden popularity of these nicotine-delivery devices has raised questions about their safety, their accessibility for young people and even whether there's the possibility of secondhand effects from the vapor.

The secondary effects that might be generated by an addiction to smell are certainly worth a whole range of explorations. After all, heroin addicts are people who like to be in a state of oblivion, so they're technically harmless, but the cost of their habit often drives them to crime. What might a scent junkie be driven to do to get that all-important scent? What would kicking scent addiction be like? Could there be an organization such as "Sniffers Anonymous?"

Additionally, we are sometimes addicted without realizing it because the "substance" may not be viewed as harmful. Are you the sort of person who cannot get going without that morning cup of coffee? Related to smell, is your house or apartment full of scents that make you feel at home, that you miss when you're away or if the scent itself goes missing? Do you have a scented candle or electronic device at your job?

Smell as an addiction can range from the simple to the extreme, depending on where you want to take your character. An aspect to consider with this etude and others is how self-aware the character is—perhaps even to the extreme of being ashamed of the addiction. In other words, is this a secret addiction? Must the character pass by a donut shop every day in order to deeply inhale, but mask it by pretending to stop at the gas station next door to check their tires? Must the woman who is addicted to the smell of a man she cannot be with solve her habit on the sly or by seeking out alternatives that are unhealthy? How far is the character willing to go to hide the addiction? How addicted are they? If the donut sniffer shows up on Monday and the shop has gone out of business, what will they do now?

On the dark side, what if the character has an addiction to the smell of fear, or to blood itself? What if the addiction is socially forbidden?

The Mighty Nostril Etude

This etude has three dimensions to it: 1) how people smell to you and how you smell to them, 2) how a character smells, and 3) a silly aspect: a smell superhero.

Okay, admit it, we've all encountered people who have a distinctive odor to them. Maybe it's someone with bad body odor or terrible breath. On "Orange Is the New Black," Nicky warns Chapman not to get too close to one of the prison guards because "His breath smells like dead things." Maybe it's a maiden aunt (are there still such things?) who gives off a delicate aroma of lavender—or sherry. Maybe it's an old girl- or boyfriend who had a very distinctive smell—good or bad—that immediately puts you in mind of them if you encounter a similar odor again. Try spending some time conjuring up a memory of anyone's particular scent—whether pleasant or unpleasant—just to see what you can recall, then apply it to a character you'd like to explore, or write about it in some other form. This is a great opportunity to get to know something about a character or lifestyle by choosing elements that you find genuinely appealing or appalling.

The Olfactory Sense

Suppose, for instance, a character always smells like mothballs, or wet dog or the heavy odor of an essential oil, and so on. Why do they smell that way? What if they're addicted to eating a particular spice and the redolence of that habit announces their presence even before they're seen? Steve Jobs would eat nothing but carrots over extended periods. His skin did turn orangey, but did he also smell like carrots and if so, what would that actually smell like? What if the character has an incredibly compelling personal scent, so that everyone who comes into contact with them practically swoons? What if they use that to their own advantage? More commonly, what if the character is a smoker? As a former smoker who became a nonsmoker and then an anti-smoker, I can assure you that cigarette smokers are big stinkers. Cigar and pipe smokers are worse. Then again, I don't mind being around people who have been smoking marijuana. You can readily tell from these simple suggestions that certain aromas will create a reaction in you. These are the things to explore because they are provocative.

Another way is to play a bit with suppositions about given characters and their particular olfactory quality. You can do this with characters you have created or with those existing in works by others.

The next time you watch a film, ask yourself what a given character might smell like. For instance, Marlon Brando's character in *Apocalypse Now* might have some kind of jungle-borne disease since he's constantly sweating and trying to cool himself off. Compare that to the likely more pleasant scent of his crisply dressed character in *The Godfather* at the opening of the film, and then contrast that with the unapologetically earthy Stanley Kowalski in *A Streetcar Named Desire*. You can do this with any actor or character—the kind of perfume Blanche DuBois would favor, for instance. Consider what scents an actor such as Holly Hunter would employ in films as varied as *Broadcast News*, *The Piano* and the "Top of the Lake" TV miniseries. I submit that a consummate professional like Hunter would investigate specific perfumes or scents to help build a character. I have no proof of this; it's just fun to think about in the same way that a costumer I once interviewed said she always starts work on a character's costume by researching what kind of underwear they would wear, given the era and their personality.

The key to this aspect of the etude is to observe the character in performance, the environment in which it takes place and so on, to develop a strong sense of what their distinctive scents might be.

You can easily do this for plays that you read or see as well. How might the stage manager character in *Our Town* smell, given that he's often portrayed as smoking a pipe? What about the two crazy aunts in *Arsenic and Old Lace*? What might the angel in *Angels in America* smell like? Huge whiffs of ozone mixed with myrrh?

Applying this notion to the characters you create can be greatly revealing of their nature. As with many of these etudes, remember that the work you do in this area may not actually show up in the script you write. The exploration outside of the story of the script can be worth its weight in character gold for you.

Conversely, perhaps your character favors a particular scent and at times you feel as if you're not really connecting with them. One solution might be to bring the actual scent into your writing space. If you're lucky enough to live in a big city, there are stores that specialize in creating scents, such as Sabon and Kiehl's in New York City. Many cities have shops that specialize in spices and even your local grocery store will do. The manager might not like you sniffing the cinnamon or Thai spice rub, but then again they might not like artists in general, so give yourself permission. Try not to place limits on how you can access exposure to scents that will be new to you.

Simply paying attention to the people around you can be a very strong exercise for opening your senses. I remember vividly the way in which the subway cars smelled on various days in New York City. In the morning rush hour, the reek of morning breath and the crazy mix of perfumes and colognes; at the end of the day, the stale smell of tired bodies emerging from confined environments; in the evening, the heady scents of people dressed to the nines going out on the town and so on. Add to these the presence of someone with serious body odor or the smell of wool coats on a rainy day, and the whole environment would change quite strongly. Now and then, I'd end up on a train where the climate control was not working, which heightened the odors significantly, especially on a very hot day.

Six Degrees . . .

None of us really spend much time focusing on odors. We mostly do it when there's something unpleasant that makes us want to move away or when we encounter something to which we are attracted. The more willing you are to experience the world through your nose, the more you may learn about how you navigate the world. By pushing the boundary lines on this, you offer yourself the chance to experience something different from your normal way of doing things.

For example, imagine that you suddenly become an animal and smell is your only way of detecting friend from foe. How would you approach smells in that circumstance? A favorite actor's exercise is to explore character by choosing an animal that somehow resembles that character's behavior, so why not do this for yourself, either on behalf of your character(s) or just for the sheer fun of it.

In *A Tour of the Senses*, John Henshaw describes a dog's ability to experience scents: "Pound for pound, dogs inhale a larger volume of air through their noses than humans do. . . . Furthermore, dogs have upwards of 200 million smell receptors, compared to the paltry 3 million allotted to humans. . . . [U]p to one-third of a dog's brain is devoted to olfactory perception."[6] Consider the results if you gave your character a doglike ability to take in smells!

The next aspect of this etude is a bit trickier: try to get a sense of how you might smell to other people. Do you use perfume, cologne or aftershave? If you asked someone who was very close to you—someone you know you can trust—to describe how you smell, what might their response be? Are you willing to hear this from them? In *A Natural History of the Senses*, Diane Ackerman cites Helen Keller describing how she could tell by the smell of a given person the "the work they are engaged in."[7] What is your work; does it create a scent that you carry around?

After all, how aware are we of our own scents? Are you sometimes nervous about how you might smell to others? Do you leap from bed to brush your teeth before your partner has to endure

---

6. Henshaw, John. *A Tour of the Senses*. (Baltimore: Johns Hopkins University Press, 2012), 119.

7. Ackerman, Diane. *A Natural History of the Senses*. (New York: Vintage, 1990), 23.

your morning breath? Do you know what they actually think about your breath in the morning? Ever asked? What kinds of products do you use to cover over the odors you believe you emanate? Bette Midler used to joke about the societal fear of so-called vaginal odor by telling her audiences that she and her backup group, the Harlettes, had "washed and shaved and FDSed ourselves into a stupor!"[8]

Are there products you use only for certain times, like getting ready for a date with someone new? Are you obsessive about it? If you are, are you aware of it? What ramifications does the obsession have? How might your obsession lend itself to a character?

The character of Andy Sipowicz on the 1990s police drama "NYPD Blue" was often shown using mouthwash or spray breath freshener. It was never commented on that I'm aware of, but the habit seemed to suggest that he was either nervous about his breath or that it was simply a holdover from his early days as an alcoholic, used to cover up the smell of booze. It was a very subtly done insight into the character with a number of possible interpretations.

We live with ourselves, of course, and our daily odors are merely a part of us. But turning our attention to these various smells can be quite enlightening. Certainly our awareness is greatly heightened when we have someone else in our environment. It may not be all that helpful to pursue this aspect of the etude from a position of self-consciousness, so give yourself a break: try to be reasonably objective.

Which brings us now to something entirely subjective and admittedly very silly: could there be a superhero named "The Mighty Nostril"? This mighty protector of the innocent might zoom in through a window when someone is going crazy putting on too much cologne before a first date. Or alert the cops to a drunk driver, noticed from miles away by their superior nose. The Mighty Nostril might descend on a town where industrial sludge has started to become harmful to breathe but is as yet undetected. The Mighty Nostril could easily detect when a volcano is about to blow or when an earthquake has disrupted a gas line or set loose a monster from deep within the earth. After all, it is speculated that farm animals anticipate an earthquake because of ions escaping from the earth, so why not our superhero?

8. Midler, Bette. "Oh-My-My Lyrics." Accessed 10 June 2014. http://www.metrolyrics.com/friends-oh-my-my-lyrics-bette-midler.html.

What if a very nervous young man always starts to sweat an unpleasant odor when he's under stress and The Mighty Nostril can arrive with his special scent to balance out the body odor? What if The Mighty Nostril can greatly enhance the scent of the roses on the nervous young man's wedding day? How might The Mighty Nostril save your life or the life of a character?

Yes, I know, ludicrous. But there's a point here: developing a character whose particular odor is a key part of what identifies them. Maybe it's a specific aftershave or perfume, or perhaps a strong scent of leather or fresh cut grass, etc.

Now, with our superhero The Mighty Nostril, what can you learn on behalf of your character about what smells provoke them? Would the scent of baby powder bring out something deeply parental in their nature, sending them into a dangerous situation to save someone? The absurdity of this aspect of the etude is intended to remind you of the importance of a willingness to play with your writing. Liberate your writing by looking at it this way: everyone daydreams; our daydreams are often just absurd reenactments of events in which we come off better than we actually did, or the person who annoyed us is punished in some colorful fashion. We don't limit our daydreams; keep the fences wide on your explorations.

Doing the Fade Out exercise for this chapter could help to build this etude for you.

Smell as Plot Element Etude

The recent horror films *The Mist* and *30 Days of Night* have used the natural elements of a storm and extended darkness, respectively, as key plot devices.

So why not smell?

Okay, it's as silly as The Mighty Nostril on some levels: "The Stink That Ate St. Louis." But why not look further? What if an evil scientist invents a substance that has the most intoxicating smell in the world yet masks tragic effects?

A recent commercial showed a woman forgiving her male counterpart's boorish behavior because his body smelled so wonderful to her. Another focuses on how a particular body spray will drive women wild. Consider, then, the comic potential in exploring this area of reaction to odor. Conversely, put some thought into the feral representation of women in these commercials and look at the dramatic possibilities. Society is never too far from a primal fear of the power of women, à la *The Bacchae* and many representations since. The limit here is only dependent on your inventiveness.

Six Degrees . . .

A different extreme comes in the form of disasters, both man-made and natural, that are related to smell and breathing. For example, the town of Picher, Oklahoma, is an abandoned city. Mining operations created instability in the land, and discarded toxic metal mine tailings (known as "chat") polluted the water and the air. Everyone moved out of Picher. Compare this to Chernobyl. Or to the town and surroundings of Sendai, Japan, that were hit by a tsunami, which in turn affected the nuclear power plant. Or the Cuyahoga River in Northeast Ohio that was so polluted it caught on fire. You don't have to go too far to find disasters that are in some way related to what's carried on the air as a result of any breakdown.

Keep in mind that the concept here is for smell to be an element, not the entire plot. It may be a minor or a major element—this depends on the story you're trying to tell and how you're using the sense of smell. Think of the hallucinogen used by the mad Dr. Jonathan Crane in *Batman Begins*. It is not the whole plot but certainly drives a very key portion of the plot.

A Faded Rose Etude

This etude is based on the functionality of the nose: your nose and your character's nose.

Begin with a simple premise that modern life is diminishing our sense of smell. Allergies and scents that overwhelm us on a regular basis can have an impact on our sense of smell or at least on our awareness of smell.

The Olfactory Sense

This etude might be both intriguing and dismaying to you. Given that the world's pollution has continued to rise to dangerous and more ubiquitous levels, city life might not be the only culprit in this regard. In El Paso, for instance, many people develop allergies because of the existence of non-indigenous mulberry trees. The trees were planted there because they're hardy enough to survive the nearly four-thousand-foot high, often scorching desert atmosphere, and because they're trees as opposed to cactuses and other growth forms. Misguided settlers to the area brought with them a love of green lawns and deciduous trees, things that are not innate to the local ecology. Result: very nice profits for the companies who make antihistamine products. Mulberries affect people in other locales than El Paso, of course; the issue is how any given plant can impact the human interface with the ecology.

Our noses are designed to take in scents, aromas, stinks and so on. Because they now have to also defend us from the amount of grit, dust, pollen and any number of airborne chemicals, our noses lose their ability to determine odors as fully as they once had when we were younger. Add to this the experience of those who smoke some form of tobacco, which also affects the senses of smell and taste, and it's clear that our olfactory organs are carrying additional loads that can reduce the full experience of scents.

For this etude, you will want to work on both your own experiences with this problem and those that might exist for a character. Seek out things that had a very strong olfactory quality for you when you were young to see whether the experience is the same or less (or possibly more).

As with the other etudes there are any number of ways to apply this etude. A starting point might be to examine a character through their experience of allergies. I have a friend who is profoundly allergic to cats and yet loves them too much to be without. As a result, she suffers an ongoing state of distress in her respiratory system. Over time this will surely have an effect on her ability to rely on her sense of smell—and it likely does now. My friend considers this a fair deal; I wouldn't, but I think I understand how she feels. If you write about a character who knowingly favors one thing over another in their sense of smell, then perhaps insights into their personality will avail themselves.

Chapter One
Six Degrees . . .

Another possibility would be to look at a character through the process of aging. As virtually all senses diminish to one degree or another, so it goes for the ability to appreciate or even utilize our sense of smell. Perhaps the diminishment is due to something that has traumatized the character in the time of the screenplay, in which case the etude could be used to trace how the lessening ability would affect the character in the future and how they would feel about the eventual loss.

A very different take would be to explore a character who is losing their actual nose, not just the nose's ability to detect scents. This offers a very grim investigation but don't take the notion too literally. What if your character was facing this loss as an eventuality; what would you learn about their sense of survival and endurance? What if the character only believes the nose will be lost? What if a character could have a full nose transplant? What impact would that have if they got not only the proboscis but the other person's sense of smell as well? Imagine the confusion and/or delights.

As all religions observe, illness and death lie at the end of our roads. Diminishment of our capabilities is inevitable. Given that, how might the lessening of scent-awareness impact the life of your character and be a factor in your plot? In film, the representation of sensory elements is relatively easy because of the camera's ability to home in on things close-up. We also accept the nonrealistic representation of things in film since modern viewers are willing to experience insertions of dream images, representations of fantasies and animated segments. In theatre these things are possible, of course, but plays are generally more reliant on language rather than visuals.

That said, something to consider for both mediums is the nature of juxtaposition, the conversations generated between the elements of a work in performance. Your character's diminishing ability might be echoed by aspects of the story—perhaps to comic or horror effect, such as if the lessened ability to detect scent is accompanied by a concomitant decrease in sexual abilities or appetite.

I encourage you to think on a symbolic level in this regard. In other words, you could explore what might happen in a play or film if the actual object with a scent itself diminishes or expands physically. The film and musical *Little Shop of Horrors* is about what

The Olfactory Sense

happens when the ravenous plant Audrey II is saved from dying by feasting on the blood of her human assistant. The plant is represented on stage by a puppet that grows in size to monstrous proportions throughout the play. This could be done for anything; an oversize clove of garlic that is giving off huge amounts of its distinctive smell could grow smaller or even larger over time and perhaps the person associated with the garlic could change size as well.

A variation on this etude is similar to those of the No Nose Etude: the ability to detect odors suddenly decreases and as quickly returns, over and over.

Let your writing process range freely over the possibilities of this etude.

★ ★ ★

There are many other potential etudes related to the olfactory sense that you may have already come up with or will invent as your explorations continue. The primary thing is to take advantage of this sense and the examinations that will greatly inform your characters and stories. The underlying spirit of all the etudes is that a writer must write and if you have no story, no ideas at the moment, at least play with the etudes to keep your mind in a creative, intuitive mode.

The following quote from Native American novelist Tony Hillerman reminds us of how critical it is to have ownership of the world we create: "An author knows his landscape best; he can stand around, smell the wind, get a feel for his place."[9]

Fade Out

An accessible way to continue experiencing the sense of smell is to keep a journal dedicated to it. This might not be something you'd do for very long but rather set as a task for a few days or a week. And you need not be terribly formal about what form your journal might take—just keeping notes on some napkins or on your smart phone is sufficient.

9. Hillerman, Tony. Quoted on http://www.quotehd.com/quotes/tony-hillerman-tony-hillerman-an-author-knows-his-landscape-best-he-can-stand.

Make a dedicated effort to take note of smells you encounter during the day, especially by seeking them out in a specific fashion. Do this for yourself and also on behalf of a given character. Focus on unpleasant smells on a given day. Take a quick detour into an alley to see what odors might be lurking there, for instance, or take a few moments to stand near a dumpster outside a restaurant or a bar, or go into a food or drink establishment just before they're open. The smell—or stink—of a bar in the morning, especially one where smoking is still allowed, will be a very vivid experience for your nose, especially if you've never experienced it before.

On another day, seek out olfactory experiences that are pleasant. In particular, try to locate aromas that you might not be quite so familiar with. Stay open to the memory-triggers these experiences might generate. Diane Ackerman writes of sitting in a eucalyptus grove with other scientists, tagging Monarch butterflies. She recalls how the strong scent was quite potent on its own but the ultimate payoff was how quickly the eucalyptus smell transported her back to childhood when Vicks VapoRub was applied to her when she had a cold.

Since it's likely that many of the smells you'll encounter could be pretty offensive, try deviating your side trips intentionally into places where you know the scents will be much more friendly and alluring. If you like perfumes or colognes, visit a store that features such products and have a "sniff-o-thon." Or visit the studio of a massage therapist, where essential oils and incense are often the operative odors as calming and healing elements.

Seek out restaurants that serve foods you may not be familiar with: Thai cooking is very distinctive from Japanese, for example, and there's a lot of variety within each cuisine. Chinatowns and the like are wonderful places to encounter a vast new array of odors. Find grocery stores that specialize in particular ethnic foods: Indian spice shops are heady experiences. If you wish to go further, try learning to cook a cuisine with which you may not be acquainted. Your awareness of the way in which the ingredients look, taste and smell will enhance your sensory acuity.

As you go through your day, keep a record of the smells you encounter. The wider the range of locales you encounter, the better, and your annotations will show this. After you've done this work for a period of time, reflect on what you've experienced. See

The Olfactory Sense

which of the scents you've encountered stand out the most. Some may suggest a story to you or a character; give yourself the space to build on that. You might even consider revisiting these places as the character and take notes on their behalf. There are so many opportunities to use this kind of work. Keep a mindful awareness of the smells, scents, stinks and aromas around you.

In other words: follow your nose.

CHAPTER TWO

Gustatory
The Feast of Living

"Nothing would be more tiresome than eating and drinking if God had not made them a pleasure as well as a necessity."
—Voltaire, author

"We write to taste life twice, in the moment and in retrospection."
—Anaïs Nin, author

The essence of this chapter is about eating and how we reveal our characters and ourselves through what we eat. It is secondarily about what we do with our mouths. Kissing is as much about taste as it is about sensual touch—especially if we break kissing down into categories ranging from smooching on a soft baby cheek to the full-out lovers' mouth meld. A further extension is the notion of taste when it refers to preference: style, life choices and so on. Our main focus will be on food; what you discover related to any ancillary aspects is the gold.

There are a number of films I think of immediately in which tasting or planning to taste food is an element: *The Discreet Charm of the Bourgeoisie* written and directed by Luis Buñuel and *The Cook, The Thief, His Wife and Her Lover* by Peter Greenaway leap to mind instantly, along with great moments like the super-sensual eating scene in *Tom Jones*, directed by Tony Richardson, and the subsequent satire of that scene in Woody Allen's early comedy *Bananas*. And who is likely to forget the fake orgasm scene at the deli in *When Harry Met Sally?*

Gustatory

We can throw into the mix more contemporary films having to do with characters being driven by a need to eat or taste that go beyond typical food, including the *Twilight* franchise or *The Hunger Games* series and the countless films and TV shows featuring zombies and vampires.

Plays with or about food are perhaps less on our radar but there are a number whose plots are hinged on the issues of sharing food, such as Thornton Wilder's *The Long Christmas Dinner*, *Dinner with Friends* by Donald Margulies and *The Art of Dining* by Tina Howe, in which a meal is actually prepared on stage. Different environments include the restaurant locales of *When You Comin' Back, Red Ryder?* by Mark Medoff or the classic William Inge play *Bus Stop*. Drinking, another aspect of taste, links us to such plays as *The Iceman Cometh* and *Cat on a Hot Tin Roof*, among many others.

Taste and tasting seem to be of greater and greater importance in contemporary life. Considering the number and variety of cooking shows and entire networks—Food Network and the Cooking Channel—it's clear that food has taken on new levels of reality and metaphor in modern culture.

Food and romance go hand in hand; consider *Chocolat* and *Like Water for Chocolate*. In John Guare's iconic work *The House of Blue Leaves*, the character of Bunny torments her lover, Artie, with a scrapbook full of recipes and photos of food, telling him she'll sleep with him all he wants but she won't cook for him until after they're married.

Tasting and our relationship to our own tastes is an ongoing life issue. Some people cannot stand to eat things with a mushy texture, for example, and seeing something on screen that presents a glimpse of such a texture is enough to make them start feeling ill. Others can't resist deep-fried concoctions, to the extent that there seems to be no limit of what can be battered and thrown into hot oil—a deep-fried stick of butter, for unnerving example.

The simple act of going to a movie theatre involves food. Movies and popcorn have long been a staple pairing—so much so that we automatically associate walking into a movie house with the olfactory pleasure and anticipated taste of fresh popcorn. And now you can have a gourmet meal at some cinemas. Theatres at every level from amateur to Broadway sell snacks that may be taken into the house, though this can be very annoying in live performance. The audience is not invisible to the actors, after all.

Chapter Two

It may well be that because we experience the world initially through a combination of touch and taste the latter has such a potent influence on us. If you're a parent, you have observed that babies will put pretty much anything into their mouths. They do this largely because it's an immediate way to experience something both as texture and taste.

As with all the senses, taste is astonishingly complex. Our taste buds can detect sweetness, sourness, saltiness, bitterness and umami. "Umami" is a tricky term to understand; essentially it refers to flavors that have a pleasant, savory taste unique from the other four qualities. Umami flavor is found in cured meats, fish, vegetables such as ripe tomatoes, green tea and foods that are fermented and/or aged, such as cheese and soy sauce. Our taste buds sense both harmful and beneficial things; all basic tastes are classified as either aversive or appetitive, depending upon the effect they have on our bodies. Sweetness helps to identify energy-rich foods, while bitterness serves as a warning sign of poisons. In addition, the tongue measures such things as texture, temperature and foods that have a perceptible coolness of flavor, such as mints, or the heat of peppers, salsas and the like.

Most people love to taste things; it's a pleasurable experience that begins with our first experience of food and continues throughout our lives. A certain percentage of people resist changes in foods or drink but many like to experiment. Going to a party or a restaurant where there will be food you don't normally encounter can be very exciting. People who self-identify as "foodies" avidly seek out the experience of new combinations of flavors and textures on a regular basis. The very best chefs continually experiment with possibilities, even at the most fundamental level of something as simple and essential as a cooked egg, as demonstrated on the first season of "Mind of a Chef," a public television show.

Beyond the films and plays that include eating as a plot device or textural element, it is very common that the sharing of food in some fashion is included in a show in order to generate a gathering-together moment. This might be relatively sweet, like the family sitting down to Chinese food at the end of *A Christmas Story*, or deranged, like a quite different family sitting down to a post-funeral meal in the play and film of *August: Osage County*.

We look at food from a personal point of view, of course. It's likely that you have stories about memorable meals or gatherings around food that went utterly awry or blissfully well. Thinking back on those stories is a simple etude you can do on a regular basis. In all likelihood you do this anyway because food is such a trigger for memory. People talk about comfort food, for instance. Mine is cinnamon toast, because that's what my mother fixed for me when I was sick or feeling blue. Someone else's was a yogurt-based mix of onion, garlic, cucumber and tomato. Quite different from mine but, well, comfort is comfort.

Conversely, the withholding or conscious manipulation of food—whether as a noble endeavor like Mahatma Gandhi's famous fasts or as punishment—creates another sense in us. An NPR report talked about something called "Nutraloaf," a tasteless concoction given in some prisons as punishment food. The report stated that this loaf (made of whole wheat bread, nondairy cheese, raw carrots, spinach, seedless raisins, beans, vegetable oil, tomato paste, powdered milk and dehydrated potato flakes) is sometimes given each day for all three meals, something prisoners have long protested. Try to imagine this experience for yourself as an alternate etude—or if you have a strong constitution, try eating only bland, unpleasantly textured food like this over a period of time.

Another familiar food-related film shtick is food flying through the air for one reason or another, ranging from the pies splatting into faces in silent films to the famous food fight in *Animal House* to the food rains of *Cloudy with a Chance of Meatballs*. What could be funnier than something we ourselves might never get a chance to see or do?

So, ahem, has this whetted your appetite?

Key Etude: Extreme Taste

You know your own relationship with food. Some foods instantly make you feel very happy knowing you'll be tasting them; others make you feel ill just thinking about having to eat or smell them. The same food may cause extreme reactions: fried liver is a delicacy for some; for others it's like a death sentence.

Build a character based on the notion that they have taste buds that are a thousand times more sensitive than anyone else's. Would they be forced into cooking for a living or into becoming a food critic? Would having a meal with less epicurean friends be a drag?

Would the character tend to faint from certain powerful tastes or experience all manner of bodily reactions—such as flames from their ears—not normally associated with food? Would extreme gustatory capacity be horrible or wonderful for your character—or both?

Experiment with what would happen if this extreme has cropped up unexpectedly. What might follow if the ability to taste things so intensely was actually painful and your character couldn't figure out how to eat anything? Imagine if one bite of popcorn would be like attaining godhood. Suppose someone in a lab somewhere was causing the sudden leap to a mega-taste or perhaps created it by accident?

The only limit with this etude is your own imagination. The possibilities are wide open. Given that, you can certainly proceed with the etude in any number of ways, guided by how far you want to carry the extremity you're granting your character. Keep in mind that pushing your character into any kind of extreme is only a way of exploring them. Often, working with an extreme condition creates an understanding of what the character is not. If you keep an open mind, however, about how you're testing the character you may find that you've widened the parameters for them. Stay open to surprises.

That said, extreme is a term that needs to be considered carefully. Some of the etude examples I have given are at the far end of the spectrum, but only based on my sense of the extreme. It would be very helpful to you to explore different levels of extreme as you see them in order to give your character or plot a very thorough going-over.

This also applies to your sense of subject matter. I have had students who could top each other in verbal gross-out jousts with seemingly no limit, while there are others in the class who can't tolerate any of it. This particular fascination may find its way to various modes of expression, such as the work of Pier Paolo Pasolini in his film *Salò, or 120 Days of Sodom* or in the play *Blasted* by Sarah Kane, both of which are pretty hard to stomach. What is your definition of this? What is your characters'?

Given that we all have 24/7 access to horrific scenes on television news, repeated endlessly on YouTube and other Internet sources, what is the limit of extreme? It has become nearly commonplace to see such horrors as beheadings and other savagery. Filmmakers seem driven to depict greater atrocities abetted by more disturbing images. What is your sense of limit to this? Where do you draw a line—if at all?

The other side of this question is this: How inured have we become to extremes in this regard? Or how much have we protected ourselves from them? I submit that we all owe it to our artistic growth to challenge the parameters of our imaginations, to strike down concepts like "comfort zone" in favor of risk and see what's really in the levels of our psyches. After all, the Greeks weren't afraid of the dark side of stuff—*The Bacchae* and *Medea*, among others, make this manifestly clear, as do creation myths in all indigenous cultures.

With all of the etudes, the idea of examining differing degrees of your characters' experiences can be beneficial to you. It may open up a character in ways that are unexpected even if you merely push them a small increment beyond their normal state of mind.

Think about yourself, for example, on a day when things are just not quite right and yet not really all that bad. Who are you on that day as compared to what you're like when everything is more or less normal, versus a day when everything is going to hell in the express lane? Now look at those days in terms of your sense of taste. Are you driven to eating pounds of sugar in all forms when you're really feeling down or anxious?

We must be willing to dig deeply into a character. It's not enough that they love their mom or are patriotic. Those are merely what I call "condition": the circumstances of the character's life at a given point in time. By exploring openly through these etudes, it becomes possible to develop characters that are not only more fleshed out but actually more like the true range of humanity all around us, thus giving rise to a greater sense of identity with them. What if the character loves their mom but mom's cooking is the worst, to the point where it's a family joke? When you start playing with what these characters are like in their most fundamental aspects they literally become people we can enjoy, relate to and more readily root for in their particular stories.

Six Degrees . . .

What would your character's reactions be to a series of different extremes? Perhaps encountering something that normally tastes very good then suddenly finding it disgusting. What would happen if the character is encountering something they used to like but now do not, yet their taste buds are suddenly in charge and they are compelled to keep eating it? Or vice versa?

What would your character do if the sudden enhancement of taste brought forward a long-suppressed memory? Imagine that on one hand the memory is exceptionally happy but linked to a lost friend, relative, lover, which flips it to a deeply tragic memory. What will this bring to the present?

The main purpose of this etude is to explore the notion of taste as an element of personality and behavior. A significant adjunct to this is the actual use of taste in the script itself. There's a moment in the film *Big* when Tom Hanks' character is at an office party and tastes caviar for the first time; he gags and rapidly ejects the food down his chin and to the floor. It's a decent comic bit because it reminds us of the immediate ways in which kids react to food and to unexpected tastes. Taste being a somewhat transitory thing, you could easily recall something that you didn't like the first time and then subsequent encounters brought a happier result. Explore a character from this perspective by looking at first tastes, second tastes and so on.

When you begin to develop a character, remember that you are working to generate a three-dimensional personality. Extreme taste can be a way of examining what a character's general attitude toward food is and how that impacts their existence. What if someone who is suffering from bulimia or anorexia suddenly develops a state in which taste has become an overriding force in their life? What if their relationship with food is virtual suicide, such as the title character in Albert Innaurato's play *The Transfiguration of Benno Blimpie*? Or that food has become fatally intertwined with gluttony, crime and infidelity as in *The Cook, The Thief, His Wife and Her Lover*?

As you read forward and consider the other etudes, place yourself in the center of the picture for a moment to ask this: What flavors/tastes do I find most compelling? Am I greatly attracted to sweet things? Salty? Do I find myself constantly craving something? This might include specific cuisines—Thai, Mexican, etc.—and it might also incorporate certain aspects of any cuisine. For example, chef, writer and TV personality Anthony Bourdain always talks about his love of pork and will eat anything that comes from a pig, including parts, categorized as offal, that most people don't especially care for or aren't exposed to in general. An entire series called "Bizarre Foods" focuses on eating things such as bugs, pork brain, donkey skin and "mixed grilled udders," just to provide a brief list. Yet many of these items are considered good food in certain environments. In some cultures every part of an animal is utilized and such complete use is considered paying honor to the animal.

An extension of this idea could go right back to character. What unorthodox taste might deepen the nature of your character?

What if the craving, sudden or not, is for alcohol? I'm always fascinated by the number and variety of bottles in a well-stocked restaurant or bar. What if your character develops an extreme taste-attachment to a particular kind of alcohol or to any kind of alcohol indiscriminately? This could be the exploration of a plot like *Days of Wine and Roses* in which a non-drinking woman (Lee Remick) marries a man (Jack Lemmon) who is a heavy drinker, and consequently follows him down a steep road into alcoholism. Alcoholism is no joke, though drunkenness has been the stuff of comedy and drama since before the Greeks, so why not explore the possibilities? You could also examine what would happen if you took the comic approach and then flipped it into drama.

No Taste Etude

The other end of the spectrum from Extreme Taste is when a character suddenly loses all sense of taste.

This can be done as a fantasy situation for the character, in order to explore the way in which they cope with a sudden, drastic loss of a key sense. Or it could be a simple shift in palate. Perhaps a person who has always been drawn to sugary foods now finds salty meals preferable, or switches from bland to spicy or the reverse. What changes might this bring about in the character?

You could also dig into this particular etude by looking at what might happen if someone purposely denies themselves a type of food or even food altogether. What if the character is an ascetic? What might you learn by exploring what has created this choice for the character?

Within the province of the etude are also characters to explore who have very obsessive relationships with food. As mentioned in the Smell etudes, Steve Jobs famously went for days at a time eating only carrots, to the point where his skin had an orange hue.

Six Degrees ...

As with all of the etudes, something you can easily add as a variant is the time of day or period of life in which this loss or state of rejection occurs. Locale could also be an intriguing twist as well; moving to an entirely new part of the globe could easily bring difficulties. Sarah Ruhl's play *The Clean House* riffs on the idea of a joke in Portuguese being untranslatable; why not look at the same issue with taste as a sort of translation? Could your character really function well on an exclusive diet of whale blubber or on real "Thai-hot" spice levels of Thai food?

Imagine that your character is a twentysomething about to have a first meal with the family of a significant other and that the family is comprised of gourmets. What might happen if the character loses all sense of flavor and only experiences texture? What would happen if the character were to judge a chili competition or a bake-off? There's no limit to the possibilities of what a sudden loss of taste would create.

Then again, suppose you were the person in that circumstance? Imagine eating your favorite food, starting from visualizing how great it looks and how wonderful it smells as you remember it, then take a bite with all taste abruptly eliminated. What would the experience be like? Some people, with occasional justification, have described certain health foods as having the texture and flavor of wood shavings. What if that suddenly happened to you with any food you tried?

Think also of what would be the next step? Would there be a doctor in your character's world who specialized in working with the lack of taste? What if there was a doctor who could do a tongue-replacement surgery that would completely restore the sense of taste but your character would face having to relearn how to talk? What if the transplanted tongue retained the donor's taste buds?

The point, as with all these etudes, is to keep on playing with the tool that we writers have, the magical "what-if?" What if your character loses all sense of taste, finds that doctor, relearns language only to find there's nothing worth talking about except food and becomes such a bore about it that no one will talk to them or eat a meal with them?

What if, in seeking a state of no taste, the character develops extreme sense reactions in other areas, such as painful hearing ability? What if the character happens to hit a magical level of asceticism and becomes a demigod?

Following the path generated by the "what-if" can lead to many possible plot avenues. Your willingness to follow these tracks is where this process can truly be helpful to you.

Writers must write. Even more than that, writers must daydream. I don't know how someone comes up with something as powerful and vast as Dennis Potter's original BBC television opus "The Singing Detective" without tapping courageously into their fantasies. I don't know where Samuel Beckett or Adrienne Kennedy found their plays except in the landscape of their wandering minds. In sum, don't fear the extremes of your imagination; challenge the boundaries you perceive and tear them down.

Ritual Meal Etude

Several decades back, a friend was about to leave New York for Los Angeles, hoping to break into screenwriting. I told her I would cook her a meal that I hoped would bring luck. I knew she liked fettuccine alfredo, so I made that with the fresh ingredients only a city like New York can provide and I also made broiled lobster tails. It was a great meal, with some outstanding white wine, and I sent her off into the night, via taxi, to her apartment and her transition to L.A.

Years later, she achieved much success with her writing, winning major awards. We'd lost touch by then but you can believe that my meal and I took credit for her achievements—at least in my mind.

So then, what would you think of as a ritual meal for someone? How would it change if that someone was a casual friend versus a potential lover? Or if it was a difficult relative or someone you wanted to please for a job?

Or what if it was someone's last meal?

If you choose to explore a character and/or plot based on this etude, you will find that your understanding of the circumstances is immediately challenged. Who is your character trying to please? How far are they willing to go to make this person happy (or satisfied, or mollified, etc.)? Does your character understand enough about the other person in order to come up with something that's actually great? Does your character unthinkingly choose a meal that they once prepared for a former lover or spouse, only to realize it as the dishes are about to hit the table? Are there biases in the choice your character makes, based on a lack of understanding of the other person's lifestyle? Would your character understand how to pull together a kosher or halal meal? What if the guest is vegan and your character is normally all meat and potatoes?

Six Degrees . . .

As you can readily see, the possible complexities of the etude are pretty extensive. You can further complicate it by investigating the level of competence in your character to prepare or order the meal. In the film *Kramer vs. Kramer*, the first time Dustin Hoffman's character tries to make breakfast for his son is an absolute disaster. Some of this is because Hoffman's character isn't much of a cook but the additional complication is that he's trying to please his son by trying to make the same breakfast his ex-wife used to make. You can easily spin obstacles for your character in virtually uncountable directions. Though I was comfortable in a professional kitchen as a prep cook, the day I took over as the lunch cook was a series of small and large disasters, and many burns.

Perhaps you could begin with considering what you would like someone to make you for your idea of a perfect meal. My dad loved orange cake. He only wanted it once a year, on his birthday, and my mom would make it for him (I just got a lovely whiff of it while writing this). I never thought to ask him why he wanted it just that one time of the year. I don't think it was very hard to make—it was a pound cake with grated orange rind and flavoring and a bit of icing—but it seemed to be something he only wanted that one time. Looking back, it clearly had some particular meaning for him and now I really wished I'd thought to ask. Regardless, that was a perfect birthday treat for him.

What kind of remembrances might your character wish to celebrate? Birthdays, graduations, yes, but what about darker things that are more commemorations than celebrations, like the breakup date of the character's first true love or the day they got away with a theft or a murder or even worse? We can do well for ourselves if we keep a very broad sense of what it is people might want to acknowledge, especially by avoiding clichés. What is it that your character finds meaningful, what's in their memories—how do they ritualize these things?

Keep in mind that the word "ritual" goes easily hand in hand with eating, so you don't have to stretch too far. Think of a birthday or wedding or funeral that has not involved food in some manner just for starters.

What if your character is stuck somewhere and cannot get to the foods they love? Jail, a desert island, the moon—anywhere will do. What might they do? Would they plan a menu over and over, adding bits and pieces to make it more and more ideal? In Manuel Puig's novel *Kiss of the Spider Woman*, and the subsequent adaptations to stage and film, food in prison takes on many different meanings: as comfort, as punishment and torment, as a reminder of life beyond the prison walls and ultimately as an element of betrayal.

And, by extension, there is the prisoner's last meal. What would your character's last meal be?

Food Mood Etude

In a way this has already been touched on in the No Taste Etude, but I wanted to extend it in a different direction by focusing on the kind of emotions that can come into play over meals.

Imagine that your character is attending a meal that's badly prepared and has arrived in a particular mood that might clash with the event of the meal. Examine the scenes that might arise out of the different moods, ranging from blissful to boiling point. Imagine the same scene replayed with a series of different moods coming into play. You could have fun with this scene by keeping the same meal and choosing mood prompts out of a bag, just to see what happens.

Chase this further: What if the meal is intentionally bad? What if the person who cooked it thinks it breaks new ground but the other absolutely detests it? What if it's a first date?

The flip side of this might be a meal so great the guest falls in love with the cook, only to discover the cook can't duplicate that meal? Or what if they both discover that a magical key ingredient can no longer be found after that first encounter—the last truffle from Palau?

What if the ingredient was an aphrodisiac? What if the characters didn't know it and they're meeting about a church matter? Conversely, what if it was the only thing that made intimacy possible for the characters and was no longer available?

What if the meal was associated with a former relationship? If your character is trying to cook like their partner's mom or dad, but missing the boat, what then? What if they're trying to duplicate a recipe not knowing that your character hated it so much as a child it makes them go berserk?

Six Degrees . . .

Think back on a best or worst meal of your own experience. Really explore what the event of the meal was like. Try to capture as many aspects as you can to relive it. Once you've explored this for yourself, you might return to examining a character from this broader perspective, taking in all senses for them. For a way to enter into this process, you might jump ahead and have a look at Chapter 6, in which methods of doing sensory recall are detailed.

Food can create mood, for good or for ill. A different way to take this etude is to examine what a character might do in order to seek out a particular mood based on a meal. In *'night, Mother*, for instance, the character of Mama is a sugar fiend, always having a stockpile of junk food at hand. For Mama the treats are an important part of her sense of well-being, a symbol of "okay-ness," of a happy mood, and yet we discover she doesn't even know how to restock her treats.

In this sense, food can be part of our self-deception. Your character might plan on a particular meal being a guaranteed pleasure, only to find that it no longer has the same boost.

What foods contribute to your character's moods?

The Fine Print Etude

This is one of those etudes that seem so simplistic and yet it will reveal much about character to you. It certainly could open up some plot paths you haven't considered before.

The etude is based on a single question: Do you read food labels?

More to the point, do your characters? Do they think about what's in their food? Does it matter to them? Once diagnosed with a chronic disease like diabetes or high blood pressure, food labels become important. You will come to a related exploration, Health Etude, later in the chapter. For now, what we're looking at is the way in which your character approaches their choice of packaged foods.

In an online blog on food labeling Hemi Weingarten states: "In the early thirteenth century, the king of England proclaimed the first food regulatory law, the Assize of Bread, which prohibited bakers from mixing ground peas and beans into bread dough. Ever since, it has been a cat and mouse game between the food industry and the public (fast forward to China 2008—cheap poisonous melamine in milk powder)."[10] Weingarten's blog has many details about the progress of food labeling and/or food safety and is well worth a read. Suffice it to say that it has been a long battle to have packaged food clearly labeled, particularly with regard to harmful contents for certain people, such as amounts of sodium, sugar, gluten and so on. Restaurant chains will be required to provide calorie information starting in 2015.

For the purpose of this etude, it's intriguing to research the way in which certain foods have come into common use, especially with regard to what we regard as customary. Dianne Ackerman

---

10. Weingarten, Hemi. "A Brief History of Food and Nutrition Labeling." Accessed 2 July 2014. http://blog.fooducate.com/2008/10/25/1862-2008-a-brief-history-of-food-and-nutrition-labeling.

mentions Marshall McLuhan in this regard. He "warned us that we were drifting so far from the real taste of life that we had begun to *prefer* artificiality, and were becoming content with eating the menu descriptions rather than the food" (Ackerman's emphasis).[11]

Indeed, Ackerman provides a detailed description of what has become coin of the realm in America: artificial vanilla. "Synthetically created, this so-called vanilla was once made in part from a sulfite by-product of paper manufacturing, called vanillin."[12] A quick search for an online grocer's offering of vanilla brought up a product made from vanillin as the top hit. Is it bad for you? With all the FDA oversight, it's probably not. Is it pure vanilla? Nope.

Ask your character to consider their taste with regard to normal products used in daily life. They may be quite fine with the artificially flavored maple syrup found in most restaurants and homes. A quick look at the ingredients in one well-known "maple syrup" will show the following: "Corn syrup, high fructose corn syrup, water, cellulose gum, caramel color, salt, natural and artificial flavor, sodium benzoate and sorbic acid (preservatives), sodium hexametaphosphate."

This may be getting into a level of taste that your character might never think about. Then again, it may be the moment when a character realizes that certain tastes and/or contents are not acceptable. If they compare real maple syrup to the artificial kind, there will be a significant difference in the experience and the key to this kind of examination is whether or not it matters to the character.

An extension of this is whether it matters economically. Real maple syrup as of this writing costs about three to four dollars more than artificial. Big difference for a large family week after week, right? Then again, if you search around for price comparisons, you might come across sites in which the producers of the real deal remind you that their cost from sap to table is higher, but that their product is superior and that by buying the fake stuff, you're hurting their businesses.

The point here is that food choice, especially this aspect of it—manufactured products—can open up a lot of interesting aspects

---

11. Ackerman, *A Natural History of the Senses*, 158.
12. Ibid.

Gustatory

about character. Some people love the taste of saccharin or the like in so-called diet drinks; other people notice the presence of artificial sweeteners instantly and are as quickly repelled.

Does your character care about what's on labels? Does that change once their health has become endangered? Does it when they become a parent? Do they become more conscious once they start becoming involved with another person who is much more conscientious about reading labels and/or has undertaken a food lifestyle for their health, such as vegetarianism or veganism? How far do they go to adapt to the other or even exceed them by moving onto an even more radical diet? I once heard a story about a vegan who claimed he was perfecting his daily food intake so as to eliminate any odor in his bowel movements.

Six Degrees . . .

Then again, what if your character becomes involved with someone whose lifestyle is based on "freeganism," meaning, at least in part, dumpster diving for food. Or fall in with someone who lives on cold pizza and beer? Neil Simon did a lot with this kind of conceit when he created the Oscar character for *The Odd Couple*.

What about any character's view on ecology and their carbon footprint? Someone who has gone from merely throwing everything in the trash can to a highly dedicated recycler and composter has made a clear choice to be more aware of what happens to packaging and unused food.

There are so many avenues to pursue here, all from the starting point of insights based on reading food-packaging labels.

By extension, what other relationships does the character have with wanting to know the details about anything they consume? In some cases, it might be more than curiosity. Perhaps it's a matter of trendiness or showing off a bit. I remember a person at a nearby table in a high-end New York restaurant asking, just post-Chernobyl, whether any of the food being served had been imported from Eastern Europe. My companion and I laughed privately at what seemed to be a pretentious question but then shared an eye-exchange equivalent to: hmmmm, maybe not such a foolish concern, actually.

Chapter Two

Food Service Industry Etude

So, now we move to the other side of the taste spectrum to the world of restaurants, cafes, coffee houses and even corner hot dog stands.

Maybe you've never been a waiter or waitress but you have my word for it that it's a tough way to make a living—as is every aspect of the food industry. I have been a waiter, dishwasher, night porter, prep cook and lunch cook. I've had to scoop out the disgusting stuff from grease traps and serve people who had absolutely no respect for me as a person. I have also had the experience of preparing meals that made people happy. Regardless of the job, at the end of my shift I was an absolutely drained human being. Restaurant work is exhausting and one of the ironies is that at the end of the day workers, especially cooks/chefs, just don't feel like eating. So then, what does that do to one's sense of taste?

There are a handful of movies and plays about cooking and restaurant work. *Frankie and Johnny in the Clair de Lune*, written for stage and film by Terrence McNally, focuses on the relationship between a short-order cook and a waitress in the diner. Stanley Tucci's film *Big Night* observes contentious brothers making a sumptuous last-ditch meal to please a celebrity who never shows up.

Now, it might not make any sense to have your character do any job in the restaurant world, but this is a great way to play with the character in two ways we haven't really tapped into enough: age differences and occupation.

As a general practice, it's a great idea to craft bios for your characters. Actors who portray your characters will do this, so why shouldn't you? The more multileveled your characters are and the deeper awareness you have of the arc of their lives, the better. Seems obvious, but too many films and plays tell me the writer simply did not know how to really get below the surface. It's a good idea to keep in mind that if your script is being produced or workshopped the actors and artistic support team will likely want to know more about the backstories of your characters, so it's good if you've done this work yourself. And since we're talking about food here, keep in mind that a certain amount of process for developing a script actually takes place over meals or drinks. Sometimes, in fact, it's where the best work gets done because everyone is relaxed.

Gustatory

Suppose you want to understand a character who is a bit of a Peter Pan–type of guy. Why not explore him when he was much younger than he is in your story or go the other way by looking at him when he would be much older? We tend to forget that any story is bracketed by what's not included, i.e., the life before and after. What might the character's experiences have been if they'd been a great cook but turned their back on the business or was a lousy server whose incompetence caused a serious accident to a customer? What if your character is suddenly much older and without financial support and has to take a humiliating job working in a fast food place? Perhaps you're a young writer who has no experience with old age, retirement or the like. You can certainly learn a great deal about the circumstances by looking around at coffee shops, fast food places, bars and so on. Keep in mind that what we do as writers is to fashion truth through fiction but you can also gain great insight by talking to people about their lives.

What if your character grew up in the restaurant business? I recently read *Life, on the Line: A Chef's Story of Chasing Greatness, Facing Death, and Redefining the Way We Eat* by Grant Achatz and Nick Kokonas. Achatz came from such a background. It's fascinating to read about his young life in his family's restaurant, how his work ethic was shaped along with his palette. Suppose your character came from a household in which creating fine cuisine was part of their development? A television series called "MasterChef Junior" pits young chefs ranging from eight years old to early teens in rigorous competition.

Six Degrees...

To dig fully into this etude, see what happens if you place your character in a variety of circumstances involving food industry work. What happens if the character somehow becomes a great chef overnight through a freak accident or is a great chef who is abruptly fired? On a more realistic level, especially if you've never waited tables, explore what that job is like by observing and/or interviewing people. There are a lot of funny stories people can tell you about jobs in restaurants; there are plots to be mined.

Another variation is to explore restaurants and chefs through their cookbooks. What might happen to your character if they pursued this avenue? The book and subsequent film *Julie and Julia* is based on this concept. To take it further, assign yourself a visit to a bookstore and spend some time perusing cookbooks for cuisines with which you are not familiar. Give yourself time to read through the opening or closing chapters having to do with ingredients. Sometimes there's an intriguing exploration of historical aspects of the cuisine and the components that make it unique. Certain types of cooking—Chinese, in particular—involve a variety of techniques that one might need to master in order to make the food properly. An Indian cookbook I have used has very helpful information on where to find ingredients if you don't live in a big city. How far would your character go to pursue acquisition of a rare or extremely expensive ingredient? Would they figure out how to make substitutions of one ingredient for another or alter recipes based on dietary restrictions?

A final perspective on this etude has to do with how food consumption is related to occupation or even lack thereof. One of the interesting shifts in New York City during my twenty years there was the rise of food cart cuisine. In the early 1970s you were more likely to find only a hot dog vendor and/or a knish stand. As time went on, food carts started to offer a range of ethnic foods: falafel, Cuban sandwiches, Indian and Jamaican menus, and so on. It's typical for a busy person in Manhattan's midtown to grab something from a cart and eat it while walking, whereas with the rise of food trucks in other American cities a casual sit-down in a nearby park or on a bench is more likely.

Restaurant Customer Etude

This flips the previous etude from worker to patron. Depending on your background, restaurants may represent heaven or hell, and the same can be explored for your characters.

Perhaps you have a place where you go to eat on a regular basis. Many of us do. We find something about the place—the food, the atmosphere, the way we're treated, the prices—appealing enough that we return again and again.

Give a character such a place, just to see what will happen to their perspective when they go there. Allow them to feel at home. Provide an opportunity for their encounters with the workers and other customers to see how they function in an environment where they are very comfortable. So many possibilities arise in such circumstances. A customer may find the music the bartender selects very engaging and out of this might begin a friendship based on appreciation of certain artists or recordings. Customers hit on waitresses and waiters all the time; sometimes it actually leads to a date and a relationship.

Additionally, give a lot of thought to what having a neighborhood place means to your character. When I was a lunch cook there was a woman of retirement age who came every day. She sat by herself, simply eating—no book or newspaper—while consuming two martinis. She was friendly with everyone and it turned out that she had been recently widowed. Our restaurant had become her haven and, I suppose, the drinks her succor.

Six Degrees . . .

Some people don't know how to be themselves in restaurants and so end up acting like first-class idiots. Others don't like the fancy places because they can't relax, so they go to sketchy-looking dives because all they want is great food served hot, without any kind of pretense. There are so many choices one can make on behalf of characters encountering a restaurant, diner, etc., that you could explore all manner of eateries and find out a great deal about the people in your script. Be willing on behalf of your characters to change up the places you choose—and do this for yourself as well.

What if you're exploring just one aspect of restaurants for your character? I knew a guy whose idea of what to do after graduating from college was to drive across the country in search of the perfect cheeseburger. He claimed he'd end his quest when he found his ideal and live there. Think about all the kinds of foods that people get obsessive about—the kinds of barbecue they might favor from one locale to another, or sushi, or anything else.

What about ice cream parlors and frozen yogurt places? What impact would they have on your character at different ages? You might explore the difference in your character at a young age being exposed to previously unknown food. Is your character picky or squeamish?

Then there's the restaurant on a first date with all the confusion that may set in about ordering and who's paying the tab and so forth.

What if your character is a food critic? What if they are a chef spying on someone else's cuisine or trying to steal customers?

And, of course, what if the restaurant, bar or coffee house is where they go to write. What would the character need for that place to be like? Think of what you might learn from designing your own coffee house and the clientele.

We take restaurants for granted in many ways. We enjoy some, we dislike others; we say farewell to some because they close or the chef leaves and so on. Regardless, we have all had a relationship with a restaurant in our personal experiences, for good or ill. Give your characters a chance to encounter the same kinds of interrelationship.

Chain Food Etude

This one is a slight variation on the previous etude and as straightforward as they come. Explore a character from the point of view of what kind of chain food(s) they prefer.

As we know it's of supreme importance to the universe as to which chain burger joint has the best french fries. At least that's what the commercials have told us at times. Sarcasm aside, I have actually heard people debate this in my classroom and elsewhere at times. Perhaps they're doing it in a joking manner (no one has come to blows so far) but I can tell that there's a degree of seriousness there.

So, it may be of great concern to your character as to which fast foods they prefer, by brand or by generic choices, such as pizza or hot dogs.

By extension, your character may have a favorite chain that's not fast food per se but still a predictable menu. I visited many parts of the country on behalf of the Kennedy Center American College Theatre Festival. I was always struck by the fact that every town we went to had at least one area where the major chain restaurants were clustered like so many mushrooms popped up after a rain. At times, I had to remind myself where we were because of the similarity of these groupings.

Six Degrees . . .

As with all of the etudes, the way in which you explore any particular aspect of a character's personal choices is best created by your impulses on the character's behalf. It's well worth it to examine your own habits in all regards, to keep in mind how your choices have evolved over the years. I quit eating beef and pork in the 1990s for personal health reasons. Before that a hamburger or Chinese pork dumplings were heaven. Everything in our lives is always in flux.

Some guideline questions in this etude include such things as: What sort of cravings might your character have? Are they attached to a particular kind of flavor, such as certain soft drinks or sandwiches? Are they attracted to bland or spicy foods? How have those changed over time? What if your character has a particular wrinkle to their tastes, e.g., such an addiction to hot sauce that they have a holster with which to carry it around?

Another way of looking at this is to investigate the character from the point of view of what they'd like to have available as fast food. Who knew that now you can find a Starbucks nearly every fifty miles throughout the United States? Given that, I have occasionally wished for a chain of falafel joints across America, or sushi, and so on. What might your character dream of in this regard?

Mouth Etude

Okay, this one might be a bit delicate. The exploration here is of what your mouth likes and how you might examine this on behalf on your character.

Diane Ackerman: "We use the mouth for many things—to talk and kiss, as well as to eat. The lips, tongue and genitals all have the same neural receptors, called Krause's end bulbs, which make them ultrasensitive, highly charged."[13]

I won't get terribly unsubtle here. I'm sure you can find a thousand ways into the essence of this etude. The key is to explore what your mouth and your character's mouth enjoys other than food. It could be something as non-intimate as whistling or singing. I know

---

13. Ibid., 132.

someone who sings to themselves when angry. It's just a displacement of emotion and seems effective for them.

It could also be a full-out exploration of your character's most secret, innermost expressions of desire and passion, experienced orally.

As I discussed at the beginning of this chapter, part of our job can be to enter into the realm of our characters' extremes. Sexuality and sensuality are profoundly individual matters. It's possible that you are very well acquainted with your own feelings and actions in this regard; then again, perhaps you aren't. This is tricky stuff in America, where we are still the inheritors of Puritan ethos in one form or another. There's very little real limit, except what we impose, to the realms of desire as well as to the sometimes-concomitant aspects of shame, guilt and the like.

Body Image, Eating Disorders and Dieting Etude

Now we come to an area that can be a fascinating source of material for a writer: the way in which people deal with their weight, their body image and how they work on this in relation to food. We're still focused on taste, so keep in mind that the core of this etude has to do with food, except here the relationship is quite different because it is defined by overriding concerns.

Each January 1st sees an enormous number of people dedicating themselves to the idea of losing weight. Most people don't know how to go about dieting. They either invent crazy tactics or get involved in a program like Weight Watchers, Jenny Craig or the like. I once worked with a person whose idea of a diet was to eat a head of iceberg lettuce for lunch each day, dipping each leaf into a jar of mustard. You did not want to be on the elevator with this person any time after lunch.

How a person sees themselves and what they hope to do about it, combined with their relationship with food, can take you in a great many directions for exploration.

This can be the subject of humor, of course, but diet needs to be looked at from the perspective of what people can and cannot eat. I knew a person in New York whose diet largely consisted of forms of seaweed. They claimed it relieved their arthritis pain and stiffness.

If they thought it worked, who should argue? It's hard for most of us to imagine being on such a terribly restricted diet for our health but it exists all around us and can lead to some very intriguing considerations of character natures and choices.

The struggle that women of all ages have with body image is a common topic for popular media. Such and such star caught by the camera looking terribly overweight or dangerously thin is fodder for national gossip. Women have a greater awareness of it from the social conditioning they experience, but don't forget that everyone is capable of living in a state of denial or delusion. I have known men with bulimia, binge eating disorder and bad diet plans. Men typically tend to worry less (or maybe just do less) about body image as they age but this doesn't mean that males don't get hung up on these things.

In the current culture, physical health has become a widespread concern. More people are running marathons, hitting the gym, buying supplements than ever before. One exploration could be based on the extreme of these choices. An acquaintance became "addicted" to post-run endorphins and experienced a variety of resultant maladies—stress fractures and the like—until they caught up with the reality of what they were putting their body through.

Body image is an enormous issue for people of all types. We understand early on if we are short or "big boned" or the like, but find it difficult to come to terms with our reality. Exploring our characters from the perspective of body image can take us into some very intriguing places. Linking body image to foods and eating habits can open many doors to perceptions about the people we are creating in our writing. We're used to the notion of the detective with, say, a cocaine habit or some other wrinkle that humanizes them; why not a bulimic detective?

Health Etude

A logical partner to the preceding etude takes into consideration issues of health that have an impact on taste and eating habits.

From the U.S. Department of Health and Human Services, National Institute of Health:

The most common taste disorder is phantom taste perception: a lingering, often unpleasant taste even though there is nothing in your mouth. People can also experience a reduced ability to taste sweet, sour, bitter, salty, and umami—a condition called hypogeusia. Some people can't detect any tastes, which is called ageusia.

In other disorders of the chemical senses, an odor, a taste, or a flavor may be distorted. Dysgeusia is a condition in which a foul, salty, rancid, or metallic taste sensation persists in the mouth. Dysgeusia is sometimes accompanied by burning mouth syndrome, a condition in which a person experiences a painful burning sensation in the mouth. Although it can affect anyone, burning mouth syndrome is most common in middle-aged and older women.[14]

Although health issues are a part of all the senses, in the realm of taste the impact of dietary change can be very frustrating for someone.

There are also odd diseases that create taste issues, such as pica disorder, in which a person persistently eats substances with no nutritional value, such as dirt or paint.

The notion of exploring these maladies might be too much for you if you are easily disturbed by illness. It could be worth the visit on behalf of a character, however, who gets freaked out in the way you do. We always have to keep in mind that our characters may be the products of our imaginations, but they are ultimately entirely separate from us if they're going to have life in a production of any kind. It's good to realize this early in your career in order to avoid being precious about protecting our creations, especially in the film world. Your lovely sixteen-year-old might be turned into a crazed twenty-five-year-old if the production company decides to go there. Once you've sold a screenplay you no longer own the copyright on your script, so it's a crapshoot from that point forward.

Since this is the last etude in this chapter, it's essential to remind ourselves that we are our characters' spokespeople in a very real

---

14. U.S. Department of Health and Human Services, National Institute of Health. "Taste Disorders." Accessed 2 July 2014. http://www.nidcd.nih.gov/health/smelltaste/pages/taste.aspx.

sense. It's easy for us to judge a finicky eater in real life. When you create this picky person it's critical to have a compassionate understanding of their mental processes and history. I once teased a friend about his larder of bland foods. He told me he'd been raised by a mother who couldn't have sugar and a father who couldn't have salt. For him, nearly tasteless food was normal and he really wasn't picky about foods at all; the way he ate was just customary. That was a great insight moment for me into my prejudices and judgment.

One of the greatest forms in modern entertainment is long-form television on cable networks. When you have the opportunity to produce a series of multiple episode movies—as long as thirteen hours in "The Sopranos" and fifteen in "Weeds"—you can really dig into character lifestyle. It's impossible to imagine Tony Soprano without food somewhere nearby or Nancy Botwin without a caffeine drink.

Fade Out

For this portion, let's look at taste in the sense of choice and discrimination for things other than food. Taste as in fashion, taste as in favorite movies, books, people one is attracted to, and so on.

Your characters will be dressed by costumers, made up by hair and makeup artists, and so on. Why not play with what kind of taste your characters have in those areas as you develop the script?

By extension, as with any of these etudes, it's a good idea to explore aspects of taste in dress and the like for your character at various ages. You could also gain a lot by examining what they would choose in times of great stress or times of the happiest relaxation.

Your own awareness of taste comes into play here, of course. I'm someone who doesn't care much about clothes. I like what I like, hate wearing a tie (I feel choked by them) and prefer to be comfortable over stylish in all cases. That said, you won't find me in clothes that aren't clean or those advertising the store I bought them from in big letters (I am nobody's billboard!). Maybe you're a fan of the backwards ball cap or any similar mode of self-expression: great. What's behind that choice? How might this play into what you develop in a character?

Taste also extends to living space choices. People were a bit obsessed with feng shui a while back. It's still important to some—is it to you? Conversely, the television shows about hoarders take on the opposite sense of some form of taste—could that be one of your characters?

Finally, taste includes life choices on a broad scale. Looking around online, I noticed that there are quite a number of children's books about the senses. We may assume that a child will develop their own sense of taste in foods and clothing, but we are always influencing them in this regard while they live with us, and often beyond. A book about taste for a child offers a chance for them and us to open out to the nature of choices. In this regard, we are given the opportunity to question how open we are for ourselves and our characters related to matters of upbringing and a thousand other factors, including ethnicity, religious background and the like.

In the end, the matter of taste is really about the flavors, so to speak, that appeal to all our senses. It is the essence that gives joy to our lives. As the quote from Voltaire at the beginning of the chapter makes clear, taste may be a necessary element of human existence but thank the powers that be it's a pleasure as well.

CHAPTER THREE

Auditory
Do You Hear What I Hear?

"Hearing the blues changed my life."
—Van Morrison, singer/songwriter

"There is no such thing as silence. We are constantly immersed in and affected by sound and vibration."
—Seth S. Horowitz, neuroscientist

Hearing is the sense that runs twenty-four hours a day by necessity. As Seth S. Horowitz observes in his book, *The Universal Sense: How Hearing Shapes the Mind*, "It's the sensory system that runs in the dark, out of line of sight, telling you not so much what something is but that something important to your survival happened."[15]

We are surrounded by intersecting sonic rainbows all day, every day. Some sounds are pleasing, some not; some sounds we can't hear or can no longer hear; some sounds have been developed to disperse crowds, while others have been created to put us in the mood to empty our wallets. Some levels of film sound are designed to feed an addiction to arousal in a target audience while at the same time being loud enough to actually destroy some of the irreplaceable hair cells in the inner ear. And, of course, some sounds are those emerging from the mouths of people around us and the characters we put on stage, whether as pleasing conveyance of information, vexed disputation, poetry or song.

---

15. Horowitz, Seth S. *The Universal Sense: How Hearing Shapes the Mind*. (New York: Bloomsbury USA, 2012), 217.

Chapter Three

I chose the quote from Van Morrison because I wanted to start this chapter talking about hearing, listening and writing from the perspective of the impact of music.

As the first etude (What Do They Listen To?) will address, music is a critical part of our—and our characters'—lives. Technology has made it possible for us to have music 24/7 no matter where we are on the planet, and has given us a range of listening choices only dreamed of in the recent past. When I was a kid, I wanted a jukebox of the hundreds of songs I loved, to hear whenever I wanted. Now I have one: I keep my iTunes on shuffle, reveling as it goes from New Orleans jazz to the Beatles to a classical string quartet, sometimes throwing in a Walt Whitman or Rumi poem, just for kicks.

Music is also a hydra-headed partner to the kind of writing we do when developing a play or screenplay. It may provide support in the way of inspiration for a particular project, background sound or perhaps even a way of drowning out distracting noises from other sources. Our awareness of music as a key element of films—and sometime ingredient in plays—is very strong on the one hand and negligible on the other. We often experience a soundtrack only on a subliminal basis and sometimes even lack any awareness at all that there was music playing throughout the film. The mark of a great soundtrack is that it enhances the action without drawing attention to itself. This, as opposed to the practice of recent decades where the music is usually blasted through transitional moments—the helicopter shot of the city below, the montage of teen bliss—in order to fill nondramatic gaps while providing some commercial advantage for whatever band or singer whose music is being used.

Theatre makes much less use of emotional support music, tending mostly toward what is motivated by something in the script: a radio playing, someone singing on- or off-stage and the like. It's rare that a straight play has any kind of music at all, other than what a director might choose for pre-show, intermission or post-show, as a means to guide an audience toward the desired emotional or referential (e.g., era) realm to best experience the event of the play.

This should not discourage any writer from thinking in terms of music in their screenplay or stage play. Films are occasionally shot with a "temp score," music that conveys the emotionality without being the final choice for the finished work. Plays are occasionally rehearsed with music as an element of support and exploration.

Auditory

A question often arises in writing classes about including indications of music in plays or screenplays. I typically answer in several ways: 1) don't assume that your music choice speaks to everyone (especially the lyrics you so love, which people may not even hear as they watch the film or play); or 2) trust the song to carry the meaning of scene for you; and 3) don't price your script out of reach by saying you want such and such song by the Beatles in a certain scene—better to say that the scene should have some music with the same feeling of a particular Beatles' song.

If music for your play is becoming that important, perhaps you're moving toward writing a play that's a kind of musical. After all, modern musicals are vastly different now from the book musicals that have gone before. *Rent* performs as a book musical then morphs into a concert performance for each song, without chorus dance numbers and the like. Other musicals are virtual operas without any dialogue—referred to as "sung-through" musicals, such as *Cats*, *Evita* or the like.

Music plays such a role in our lives that it's hard to imagine a time in the world when it didn't exist, and it seems that it always did in one form or another. According to Daniel J. Levitin, author of *This Is Your Brain on Music*, "The study of the evolutionary origins of music has a distinguished history, dating back to Darwin himself, who believed that it developed through natural selection as part of human or paleohuman mating rituals."[16]

The heart of this chapter is etude work that evolves from our sense of listening, of auditory input, and music is a great starting point. We'll have a look at other aspects further into the chapter.

But before you do any of the etudes, take a moment to just stop and listen. You may be indoors or outside, you may want to move to one or the other, just to open up your receptors. I've been writing this segment of the book on a retreat with students at a place called Osage Forest of Peace, just outside Tulsa, Oklahoma. As I took a pre-lunch walk I realized I was stuck inside my head—as if I wasn't outside at all. It finally dawned on me that the trees were making waves of sound all around me in the October wind. So I stopped and really gave a listen, and got quite a concert. Do the same for yourself right now or promise it for later. And repeat as often as you can: the world is full of amazing sonic experiences.

16. Levitin, Daniel J. *This Is Your Brain on Music*. (New York: Plume, 2007), 247.

Chapter Three
Key Etude: What Do They Listen To?

Begin this etude by exploring your own musical choices and taste. Are you a fan of indie music or classical? Country or jazz? Do you listen to those forms exclusively or tend to shake things up by varying your choices?

Is there a particular music form that you absolutely can't stand? I know that some might say country, others opera, and yet most of us probably have at least one song from both genres in our mental repertoire. For example, the Everly Brothers were technically country artists, and Ray Charles released a country-inspired album (*Modern Sounds in Country and Western Music*). Both recorded a song called "Bye Bye Love," which may not seem to be country but emphatically has its roots in the style. That song has been covered by dozens of artists and it's likely you could sing along with it.

In terms of opera, many of us know at least one aria, such as "La Donna è Mobile" from *Rigoletto*, "Un Bel Di, Vedremo" from *Madam Butterfly*, and "Habanera" from *Carmen*. You may not know their names but once you have a listen you'll realize these songs have been in your head seemingly forever. Incidentally, if you watch cartoons from the 1940s and '50s, you'll hear a lot of classical music. That's a bygone practice, sadly; someone noted that those of us who grew up in those times knew a great deal of classical music because of the cartoons we watched. Who knew we were being educated while watching Bugs Bunny outwitting Elmer Fudd?

What bothers people about certain kinds of music is really interesting to think about. Opera sounds too "screechy" to some or it seems ludicrous that people only sing. Some say country music is corny, though this may depend on whether you're listening to classic country or contemporary. For others, punk, thrash metal or rap is too in-your-face, unlistenable. The question always hinges on the degree of exposure and the willingness of a given person or character to expand their range of listening. It's worth it to dig deeply into a character's background to get a sense of what their listening taste is all about. In some cases it's just a lack of exposure or perhaps too much exposure.

It could also be the result of a condition called amusia. As defined by John Henshaw in *A Tour of the Senses*, "Amusia is a term that describes a variety of conditions related to the inability to recognize various aspects of music, such as tones, melodies or rhythms. Amusia can be congenital, or it can develop as a result of a brain injury or disease."[17] Further on, Henshaw quotes writer Vladimir Nabokov's comment on his experience of the condition: "Music, I regret to say, affects me merely as an arbitrary succession of more or less irritating sounds."[18]

Similarly, what attracts people to certain kinds of music is an intriguing study as well. What do they want music to do for them or to them? What do they use it for? Is it light jazz to create a quiet background, or is it something more driving to get them dancing or making passionate love? Did your character reach a turning point in music where their taste shifted from one thing to another? Why did that happen? In the film *Silver Linings Playbook*, the Stevie Wonder song "My Cherie Amour" is an anger trigger for Pat, the main character. Perhaps your character has a song, album or symphony that is a similar trigger for bad or good memories.

Music choice is about life choices; some people grow very conservative as they age and this impacts on their taste in just about everything. Because music is almost pure emotion, the elements that affect people might become too much in time or may have arrived at a significant point of evolution where more aggression is wanted.

In any situation there is much to gain by examining your own tastes, as well as by discussing musical tastes with others. For some a night of progressive jazz is agony but others find it a truly powerful experience. Why or why not? If you're a Miles Davis fan, the leap from his landmark album *Kind of Blue* to *Bitches Brew* was a bit much for certain people, while for others, Davis' experiments with fusing rock, electronic music and jazz were revelatory.

Musical taste is very linked to background. How you are raised—there's constant music at home, there's no music at home—how you're exposed to music by friends, performance media, the Internet—how your tastes evolve as time goes on; these are all fascinating elements to consider about yourself and about any of your characters.

What Do They Listen To? is mostly a what-if game, though there's no limit on how to approach the intersection of characters

---

17. Henshaw, *A Tour of the Senses*, 250.
18. Ibid., 251.

and music. What if your character has been a longtime classical music fan who suddenly cannot stand the sound of an oboe in a piece of music—or something much more dominant and frequent, such as violins? What if they can't abide music written in a certain key? Someone once asserted that D minor is the saddest key. Perhaps, but then again Beethoven's most famous symphony, the Ninth, is in D minor, and is hardly a downer. Mahler's Ninth is in D major, shifting by the end to D-flat major and is a meditation, at least in part, on what for some is the ultimate bummer: death. If you look at other works by composers in those keys, you may find some that are not pleasing or very pleasing to your ear. How might this play out for your character?

What if your character develops a syndrome in which they must race from one type of music to another throughout the day? If you've ever been in a car with a compulsive radio-button puncher, you know the type and you likely know the degree of irritation this may have caused you. Perhaps the character suffers from some kind of emotional or mental malady that urges them to keep seeking different kinds of musical input. Maybe they experience voices telling them to find variations in songs. Perhaps they are just looking for the right musical "score" for their day. After all, music is portable and we can create our own walking-in-the-park theme by what we select. You can push this notion even further. In the 1990s, on the series "L.A. Law," Kevin Spacey played an eccentric, wealthy character who traveled with a trio of female backup singers, in case he decided to break into song, which he often did. Many of us have our soundtracks; what might the choices be for your character? What if they wanted to be accompanied everywhere by a brass band or somebody playing a conga drum?

What if your character abruptly turns into such a rabid fan of a particular form of music that they absolutely must quit their job and follow the band around? This happened to a number of people with the Grateful Dead. The band became a lifestyle, if not an obsession.

Everything is a matter of degree, of course. The key to your explorations is to put the character into a dramatic environment where they are interacting with another character, giving you a chance to explore the voices of the people you're interested in, as well as immersing yourself in their visual world through action

Auditory

narrative. You could also use music during your writing sessions as a way of setting tempo for a scene or even for the rhythm of a given speech.

Simple choices like having characters argue about music can open up many doors for your understanding of a given personality. Using a dispute as a foundation can be very empowering for your creative work, provided you present a conflict in which either side can win. Once you launch the issue it's exciting to see how far your character might go to win, what kind of tactics they will use (this changes wildly depending on the gender, background and relative age of the characters, provided you're being truthful and realistic about a given character's tendencies), and what their ultimate goal is. Some people just want to win a feud and will do anything to be victorious. Some people are interested in seeing how their own thoughts get expressed in a heated discussion as well as hearing the other side, sometimes even asking someone they really trust to play devil's advocate. Other individuals are conflict-averse, which might leach the drama out of your exploration, though it could reveal a far subtler means of addressing an issue.

Six Degrees...

Further explorations can certainly include writing about the character's family background, both to discover the kind of music and views about music the character was exposed to as a child and to have a look at your character at a younger age than that of the script. The opposite of this is looking at how their taste in music changes as the character ages. A lot of us baby boomers still love rock and roll, so-called "classic rock," but also enjoy current music, so be wary of assumptions.

What if your character suddenly discovers a new form of music that's radically different from what they had been accustomed to and it changes their lifestyle entirely? People in the 1960s reacted in highly positive ways to the psychedelic music of Jimi Hendrix or Pink Floyd, or the raw energy of the Velvet Underground. This included individuals who had previously considered their tastes to be conservative; perhaps something dormant had suddenly become active in them. The punk movement of the 1970s and '80s brought a lot of people into a new way of looking at their lives, at performance and a number of other things. MTV and other media introduced the range of hip-hop forms to a broad audience.

What changes might music bring into your characters' lives that they simply had no expectation of experiencing? The opening scene of *Talk to Her*, by Pedro Almodóvar, shows a man so moved by the music and dance performance he's witnessing that tears are rolling down his face. This leads to the start of a friendship that eventually leads to different tears, all from the impact of the performance being experienced by the characters.

In the film and play *Amadeus*, Mozart's music is foregrounded. Salieri's detailed description of Mozart's Serenade for Winds, third movement, helps us hear what we perhaps had not noticed before and brings a deeper understanding of how Mozart's music works. It also shows us Salieri's powerful recognition of Mozart's genius, while revealing his agonized awareness of his own mundane talent. What if your character is a musical genius or savant?

The technical aspect of music does not matter to most of us—we like it, we don't like it, and it stops there. Suppose your character has an extreme awareness of the technical aspects of music, such as an extraordinary critic. What would their experiences of listening be like? What if they had perfect pitch? Would listening to music that's even the tiniest degree out of tune or created with the Auto-Tune software drive them absolutely crazy or would they see the flaws in the making of the music from a more Zen-like perspective?

Who is this person you're creating? What's their personal relationship with music and how does it manifest in their day-to-day life?

What if they suddenly lose their hearing? Have you ever thought about what might occur if you were suddenly deprived of one sense or another? Has your character? What if the fear of this is the point of the exploration rather than the literal reality? When author Seth S. Horowitz interviewed Dame Evelyn Glennie, the world-famous percussionist who is mostly deaf, he asked her to define what music was to her. Her response was that it was something "that you create and listen to with your whole body, not just through your ears."[19]

Ultimately, music is a highly individual matter. How does your character use music? Is it their habit to play new age music or

---

19. Horowitz, *The Universal Sense: How Hearing Shapes the Mind*, 135.

electronica in order to unravel a hard day, or is the preference for thrash metal to wall the day out? Do they have to listen to only one station when they're driving to work or have a mix CD for the trip? A very dear friend at one delicate point in their life began listening to one song (Lou Reed's haunting, ironic "Perfect Day") over and over while driving places, nearly sending their roommate to the asylum.

A further extension of this etude is to look at how music might be made by your character. This is a way of moving your exploration on behalf of a character into something proactive and acknowledging the fact that we are all capable of making some form of rhythmic, if not lyrical, expression.

As children we participate in creating rudimentary music through rhythms. Kids like to bang on things; they like to move to the influence of music, long before they're capable of understanding language. Every time I've gone to Australia for a conference, I've witnessed groups of Aborigines making music and dancing, welcoming us visitors to their land, which is a very moving concept. They performed their traditional ritual dances accompanied by several didgeridoos and some rhythm instruments. I had never been exposed to live indigenous music before, other than Native American; I realized what I experienced was nearly timeless in origin and universal, simultaneously. How would your character react to something like this? Do they explore music from other cultures? How do they go about it, if they do? I remember there being a split between people who thought that Paul Simon's *Graceland* album was a great fusion of western and African music versus those who saw him as the equivalent to an exploitive imperialist.

Another variation takes in the ability to make music via computer applications and software. There are so many possible ways of creating music through our electronic devices it seems as if anyone can write songs or even symphonies. It has become commonplace for people to create solo albums without using actual instruments, something that was unthinkable not long ago. It's easy to explore a character who is already familiar with the technology; what might happen if you bring a character into contact with the tools to do this who isn't so familiar? I recall a story about a group who placed some laptops in a third-world village, without any instruction on how to use them. The kids in the area figured them out in no time.

I have friends my age and older who navigate the Internet with aplomb, though it's mostly to post pictures of the grandkids. Even so, if your character is very old, how might the ability to make music on their computer impact them? Might it somehow ease the extremely trying effects of Alzheimer's? An entry on the Mayo Clinic website suggests that this can be true. The site also suggests that this can be valuable for others as well: "Music can also benefit caregivers by reducing anxiety, lightening the mood and providing a way to connect with loved ones who have Alzheimer's disease—especially those who have difficulty communicating."[20]

Regardless of how you approach the variables within this etude, the key is that music is directly linked to emotions. In the film *Her*, Theodore tells his portable music system, "Play melancholy song." When the choice isn't right, he says, "Different melancholy song." The beauty of the moment is in the choice of the word "melancholy." In the world that Spike Jonze created, Theodore—and presumably the people around him—focus less on what song as opposed to what kind of song. How would your character approach these kinds of choices?

Sound Invasion Etude

It's a noisy world out there. Cities can be absolutely cacophonous. Taxis, subway tunnels, rush-hour traffic, cars with the entire trunk filled with speakers blasting the mortar out of brick walls, cell phone shouters—all elements of daily life in the city. The country can be a clamorous place as well with the roar of farm machinery, bird song, the nightly soundings of frogs and insects, and these days with the whir of wind farms or the incessant uproar of fracking: drilling, burn-off flaring, truck traffic and generators going 24/7.

This exploration looks at how your character interacts with sounds that are not of their choosing.

The start of this etude is actually linked closely to the next etude, Familiar Sounds. The key in the Sound Invasion Etude is to look at

---

20. Smith, Glenn. "Alzheimer's Disease." Accessed 12 July 2014. http://www.mayoclinic.org/diseases-conditions/alzheimers-disease/expert-answers/music-and-alzheimers/FAQ-20058173.

your character within their home environment, where in Familiar Sounds, the environment is in a state of shift.

Imagine your character on a quiet evening in their house or apartment. If you begin from their preference for their domestic soundscape, you'll discover aspects about them that may be useful for other kinds of exploration, possibly linked to the What Do They Listen To? Etude. You can explore an entirely different direction, however, by examining what may be part of their home world that has nothing to do with music. At this moment I have an air conditioner humming away in the background and from time to time the pull chain on the ceiling fan knocks up against one of the blades. It's a late summer evening so there are nocturnal noises outside—frogs and crickets—but also neighbor sounds, such as the guy who likes to work in his garage.

Spend a few moments listening intently to your space. If there's music or a television on, turn them off and just breathe in the sound through your ears. What do you experience? What might your chosen character experience in their environment? I live in an isolated apartment in Tulsa, a medium-size town; my neighborhood is very suburban and usually very quiet. When I lived in the East Village of New York City, the soundscape in my apartment and outside (and all around, since it was a six-story building) was radically different from where I currently live. Even so, we adjust to the sonic atmosphere in which we dwell, so in time I really didn't hear the fire trucks rolling out from the station down the block, or perhaps only heard them as an echo.

Spend some quality time with your space and then give your character the same chance to be fully settled into their domestic normalcy. Out of sheer impulse, invent something that bursts into their place's soundscape and shatters it, if only for a moment. There are so many possibilities in this kind of scenario, ranging from human-generated noise to machine-created sounds. Write the scene paying close attention to how your character reacts. Some people have extremely sensitive hearing and a very low startle threshold, making a sudden loud noise actually painful to their ears and body. Others are a bit more prone to absorb and move on.

Take care to appreciate your character's innate qualities, both mentally and physically. Someone who has experienced trauma handles sudden sonic intrusions with great difficulty. This might be an aspect of their thought processes and it also could be that their body has become a resonator they can't control. I once had a deep cut on the bottom of my foot and resultant stitches. The night after the accident I attended a fireworks display and was shocked to find the stitched wound painfully vibrating from the explosions. That was a relatively small trauma; how might someone react who had more serious complications?

In addition, you can look at the character's reactions based on someone intentionally making the sound incursion. Character A is very sensitive and Character B thinks popping a balloon behind A's back is hilarious. What ensues? Imagine the variety of scenarios to explore from someone being intentionally invasive with noise. Play with their motive: to tease, to shock, to provoke, seduce and so on.

Six Degrees . . .

Pick a place other than home where your character is a regular. It doesn't need to be a quiet place like their dwelling. All you need to do is examine what happens when sound suddenly blasts into the space and how the character reacts. Even in a noisy bar an abrupt explosion of sound—a speaker shrieking feedback—can overwhelm and even completely disorient. An excess of sound can actually cause people to become dizzy and even nauseous. What kinds of reactions might your character have? Be mindful that the term "invasion" doesn't have to mean something sudden or even threatening. I have a favorite coffee house where I like to read and write; it drives me crazy when people come in and talk in loud voices, completely changing the atmosphere. This is when invasion means interruption or intrusion; nonetheless, it's annoying and we experience this all the time in such a range of ways it's a bit mind-boggling.

There are so many possibilities of how you can look at the notion of invasion. Perhaps it isn't simply sound but the arrival of someone who talks without a seeming end point or punctuation. Maybe it's the sudden appearance of a person who is crying uncontrollably or arriving with a child who's distraught. Sit loose to the variations you can come up with. It's likely that your character will tell you about the kinds of things they find intrusive as you explore their relationship with sound. Conceivably the sound itself may introduce or engender a character you'd never considered before. After all, actors do animal exercises on a regular basis to develop a physical sense of character; who's to say that a related exercise in which they explore being a sound or an instrument of some kind might not provide similar results? Miles Davis once said he liked a muted trumpet because it most closely resembled the human voice. What about the character whose strident voice is like an unmuted trumpet?

Familiar Sounds Etude

As mentioned in the preceding segment, this etude is related to the invasive nature of noise but on the flip side: sound as comfort element or at least as a sense of the familiar.

The process for this exploration is to keep track of the sounds that are part of your, and then your character's, daily experience. This includes sounds you are aware of, seek out or are a natural element of your environment that provide a kind of underscore to your normal routine. As Seth S. Horowitz observes: " . . . every city has its own background noise signature."[21] So, too, does everyone's home, car, office and so on.

Most days begin with an alarm going off to wake us up. Many of us think the snooze button is the greatest invention of all time and can keep hitting that thing for cycles on end. My clock has an alarm but also a radio function with a separate setting. After I've smacked the snooze button a few times, NPR comes on, telling me all about what's been happening while I've been conked out. Once I roll out, there are dozens of sounds that make up my morning even before leaving for the day.

Take particular care to listen deeply to your normal day. I realize that not everyone has such a thing as a predictable, regular day, but keep the parameters on this notion loose and you'll find a lot of great stuff. Track your day via sound, all day long if you can. Include everything you can notice from how your car sounds starting up,

---

21. Horowitz, *The Universal Sense: How Hearing Shapes the Mind*, 40.

all the noises around you in your work day, your chewing sounds and chatter at lunch, and so on. Don't be afraid to be as minute in your observations as you can because this is where your best work for your character can come into play.

Once you've experienced this day, whether with notes or just by observation, do the same for a given character.

Six Degrees...

By extending this etude, you will afford yourself the opportunity to generate a fully realized world for the person you're creating or reexamining. For instance, if you're writing something in a historical time period, having a sense of what that world's sounds were or might have been can greatly assist in fleshing out a character. Too often plays and films that are period stories ignore the fact that the characters in those eras actually lived and had experiences just like our own but for the differences in the environment. In the film *Shakespeare in Love* we experience the sonic landscapes of the marketplace and pubs, the splatter of chamber pots being emptied right onto the street, the kinds of music and ritual sounds that accompanied royal events, among others.

As you create the sonic experience of your character, remember that what may have been familiar on a certain series of days might shift into new sounds with the arrival of environmental change. It's typical in a city like New York to find the street where you live being torn up in the morning or scaffolding going up across the street. These sounds begin as unfamiliar but can quickly become part of the aural landscape for your character.

You can always extend this into familiar sounds as nostalgia. Familiar sounds as nostalgia for your characters can include sounds that were just part of the place and time. A pleasantly squeaking rocking chair, the sound of lawn mowers, a cat purring, an infant's breathing in sleep and all the lovely, often incidental, sounds that create our relationship with the world. Music instantly propels us back in time, of course, being very linked to memory.

Daniel J. Levitin raises some interesting questions: "How are memories of music different from other memories? Why can music trigger memories in us that otherwise seemed buried or lost? And how does expectation lead to the experience of emotion in music?"[22] He begins the answer to his questions by stating, "Tune recognition involves a number of complex neural computations interacting with memory. It requires that our brains ignore certain features while we focus only on features that are invariant from one listening to the next."[23] We're not aware of this while it's happening. The notion that our brain ignores one aspect in order to favor another is at the heart of why we seek out familiar sound.

It's likely that as you explore your day and/or your character's, you'll recognize sounds that go unnoticed for the most part. This is where the idea of comfort comes into place; the sounds are as much a part of the character's familiar world as is the furniture, the posters on the walls, coworkers, cooking smells and all the savory bits of life.

The next layer to this would be to push the notion of comfort to a level that is perhaps a bit abnormal, if that will serve the character or if it will stretch the character in some fashion. Given the nature of character X, what might they find comforting that could be quite different from any other being? In the animated character Shrek we have a personality that thrives on grossness; who knows what possibilities of sonic input he would find comforting? And what if that which we perceive normally as peaceful becomes inverted? In the Martin McDonagh play *The Pillow Man*, the main character, Katurian K. Katurian, might find the quiet of his jail cell deeply threatening since it only represents a state of pause before the next brutal interview.

As with any etude, your character's sensitivity, your willingness to push things to an extreme, and the genre in which you decide to place the character can all have a huge impact. There's no reason why a character in a comedy couldn't move through a landscape they find familiar but we would find unbearable because the sounds and the conditions are so crazy or threatening or somehow past our sense of acceptability. An example of this would be in the animation/live film *Who Framed Roger Rabbit?* The existence of myriad cartoon characters and their related sound effects are just a natural

22. Levitin, *This Is Your Brain on Music*, 133.
23. Ibid.

part of a very unpredictable world, one where we might find it impossible to live, though fun to visit.

If you're of an experimental nature, playing with sound, either as invasion or familiarity, could be of great value to your creative expression. In the performance piece *Savage/Love & Tongues* co-created by Joseph Chaikin and Sam Shepard, music instruments created from an array of commonplace household items were used to create the soundscape that underscored the production at the Public Theatre. A character in a film or play who communicates through noises or sound (even nonverbal music) has intriguing potential. An animated short called *Gerald McBoing-Boing: Jolly Frolics*, about a boy who communicated through sound effects, won the Academy Award in its category in 1950 and saw life again in various iterations as a series in the '50s and in 2005. The short is available on YouTube. In the play *Idioglossia*, which was eventually made into the film *Nell*, the main character is at first considered mentally challenged because she does not speak in any conventional language. Eventually it's discovered that her speech is a combination of her mother's impairment—she'd had a stroke that paralyzed one side on her face—and a private language Nell had developed with her late sister in their profound state of isolation.

These examples might not fit your image of sound usage, but what sorts of ideas emerge when you consider the possibilities? What may be familiar for one—such as a language no one else speaks—may be utterly alien to another. What defines a comforting or predictable quality or level of sound has so many variables you could play with this etude for days on end. You could even try tracing this back, even if only as an imaginative exercise, to what you could hear while still in the pre-birth state. Your mother's voice would predominate over any other sounds but what else might have been present? People have bought into the fallacious claim that playing Mozart near pregnant bellies could help boost their child's IQ or make their baby happier or any number of other notions that have been debunked. Still, it's easy to see why this notion would seem to be true; after all, most of us choose some form of music or sounds as comfort and reassurance. Do we do so because we remember pre-birth music? What those earliest memories are for your character will reveal a great deal about them at every level of their emotional states.

Sound Shift Etude

This is a very different kind of etude, in that it asks you to think about how you determine sound quality for your environment and how a character might do the same. It might even provoke you to reassess your various spaces in a physical fashion.

The essence of this exploration is based on your preference for sound in your daily environments—home, office, while in transit—and how you work with that preference. The focus is on experimenting with shifts in sound on behalf of your character based on things that are reasonably within their control.

At the simplest level, the etude is about where you put your speakers and where your character might opt to do so in their environment. It's also a way of having a look at how your character relates to music in terms of their sound system. Are they the sort of person who is perfectly okay with a cheap set of speakers whose bass sounds are essentially hollow thuds? Are they the sort of listener who always look for the best possible reproduction of music? Are they someone whose sense of hearing and taste in sound is in steady evolution? Or devolution?

Just to give you an idea about this, I encourage you to go online to do some pretend shopping for speakers and pay close attention to the reviews, especially the lowest ratings. It's very intriguing to read through the commentaries on different qualities of speakers. As cost goes up, so do the demands of the purchasers, who fill their reviews with analyses that are almost incomprehensible to the average person. One assumes these audiophiles know what they're talking about, of course, but such reviews might be too daunting or confusing for the average individual and therefore not terribly helpful. Some of the reviewers are also incredibly picky, which can provide a character study for you to play with. As you no doubt know, reviewers on certain sites provide names and a link to other reviews by them. This is great stuff to peruse and true in any area for online shopping, restaurant and hotel reviews, and so on. Some people are so into their preferences and demands that they complain about the most phenomenally picayune things (of course, this doesn't include you and me).

So, then, how dedicated is your character to sound quality? I recall meeting a guy who was so serious about his sound system that his turntable was mounted on a concrete pedestal that went through the floor to the ground. He had massive speakers and a bank of amps and preamps that could have served as the inspiration for a dozen sci-fi films. And what did he listen to? Mostly sound effects recordings: "Man, that train sounds like it's coming right through the living room, doesn't it?" he exclaimed, while pulling out a bagpipe record.

The other element of this is where the character might choose to place the speakers in their space. If the character is especially sensitive to sound, the placement of equipment could easily be a long experience of trial and error. Are they the sort of person who will rearrange time and again until they're happy with their space and setup? Are they willing to introduce physical elements into the environment to help make the sound that much better, such as sound baffles or a new rug? Improvements made to Alice Tully Hall in New York's Lincoln Center are legendary. It was a recital hall with the reputation for terrible acoustics and now, with adjustments, boasts some of the very best. Would your character shift their plants around, buy a different coffee table or put cork squares on the wall to improve the sound in their space? Would the arrival of a flatmate, partner, in-law or any other added personality impact on this?

Six Degrees . . .

If music doesn't matter to your character, you can certainly explore a different aspect: their television sound system. If your character is a fan of action films, having that big bass sound for explosions, car chases and the like can be critical when they choose a system for their movie watching. After all, we're in the era of heightened digital quality at every turn, so even people who don't long for the helicopter landing to sound as if it's right in the living room are being treated to high-end quality.

That said, it's always intriguing to go to a store that sells these systems and into the room where the acoustics are ideal to have

Auditory 73

stuff demonstrated. It's rare for the system to sound as good at home, of course, and this might be a really interesting visit with your character: how do they cope with that which is promised versus how it actually turns out? Examining your character's coping skills is fodder for all of the etudes throughout the book.

A way of playing with this etude is to look at the character's home environment in a way perhaps you hadn't considered previously. How much time do they spend just listening to music or watching television? Is their space set up to be ideal for those choices? Do they live with another person who doesn't really want their living room to be a home theatre bristling with speaker stands? Does the character have such a passion for music that they have their system wired up throughout their dwelling?

How unique is the world of sound where they live? I once spent time with friends who lived in a mansion where nothing short of Altec Voice of the Theatre speakers, which stood about five feet tall, could pump enough sound to fill the massive living room (the fireplace was big enough to actually walk into—picture the Florida mansion in *Citizen Kane*). Cranked up, the sound could rattle your rib cage.

Another element is headphones. We've gone from the clunky ones of the 1960s to the super lightweight iPod sets to earbuds to the ones that look like fat marshmallows or provide noise-canceling quality, and who knows what's next—speaker implants? What type might your character prefer? Some people like the noise-canceling type of headphones for travel or even to block out sounds in their work environment. The headphones reduce ambient noise through a process called "active noise control," a means of reducing unwanted sound by the addition of a second sound specifically designed to cancel the first. Having used the noise-canceling ones on long flights, they're not my preference for normal listening; something about having sweaty ears is just entirely too strange. In addition, how important is sound quality for your character in this regard? It's not unusual to see singers with some form of headset when they're fronting a loud band.

Another aspect of this is where the character uses the headphones. The obvious is while in transit in one way or another: subway, walking, bicycling, etc. In the traveling environment, what is the relationship with the headphones in terms of style, volume and what the character is listening to, such as music versus spoken word material? How intrusive are other sounds in the environment? Does your character keep their headphones cranked up so high everyone on the bus can hear the music? Is the character someone who would wear headphones while driving and ignore the risks involved with blocking out a crucial sense? What do any of these choices reveal about the character for you?

Keep in mind that it's always possible for a basic exploration to take you to unexpected places. Talk to others about their experiences in this regard. It's likely they'll have stories for you that will open additional doors.

Speech and Hearing Etude

This etude is not going to be technical. I don't have enough background to go too deeply into the ways in which our production and reception of sound are affected by illness, trauma and the like. The core of this is much more for us laypeople. That said, there's much to be learned from talking to people who specialize in treating speech and hearing issues.

The point of focus in this etude is how we talk and how we listen to others talking. The way we shape sounds with our mouths is based on a wide variety of factors, including regional dialect and physical trauma.

The issue of writing dialect often comes up in classes. Students want to know if they should write phonetically for a character and if so how much or how little. I try to steer them away from writing in phonetics since it can look like Klingon on the page. Instead, I encourage them to look for key words or phrases that capture the idiomatic quality inherent in dialects. A friend's grandmother, a very proper lady, would never stoop to base language but when she got mad enough she'd bark out "shoot a monkey!" The flavor of that, combined with her deep Mississippi accent, would likely be enough for a trained actor to get a handle on how to approach that dialect.

In order to create the speaking manner for a character, it will be helpful for you to begin with yourself and then expand from there, especially if you can do first-person research, going beyond dialect recordings. In the South, everyone tends to say "y'all." In

Oklahoma, however, I sometimes hear what sounds like "y'ah." At various places in the United States I've heard such variations as "youse," "you'uns," and the like.

Start from the way in which you speak. Where are you from? Where did you grow up? Have you moved around a lot or lived in the same place your entire life? Whose way of speaking has influenced you? How aware are you of how you speak? I grew up in Baltimore where the dialect is very different from anywhere else in the United States except in the areas of southern New Jersey and Philadelphia. As a budding actor I worked hard to get rid of my flat sounds and dropped syllables ("Balamer" for Baltimore; "amalance" for ambulance; consult http://www.baltimorehon.com/ for more examples and variations). It helped a great deal to be able to mock the sounds by exaggerating them because then I could hear the difference. I could also sense how my mouth was shaped when I spoke in "Balamer-ese" as opposed to standard American.

Geography still plays a great role in the way we speak. This is true in America but globally as well. If you've never read or watched *Trainspotting*, for example, you'll find it very intriguing to encounter language that is quite different from standard Scottish, let alone English. Any actor who has had a range of experiences will tell you that learning a midlands accent versus cockney or posh London is quite a challenge. I understand a fair amount of Mexican Spanish; can't follow speakers from Spain at all.

Six Degrees . . .

After you consider your dialect heritage, something else to think about is the kind of language you use in your various modes of communication. My example with students is: "What is the difference between what you tell your parents about coming home at three a.m. in a less-than-optimal state of sobriety, as opposed to what you tell your friends the next day?"

Language is situational. Language is self-referential. Language can be nonverbal in the sense of someone's tone of voice or any threatening sound. We are partly pre-programmed in this regard and partly develop reactions from experience. Seth S. Horowitz comments on the animal world with regard to listening as a matter of survival: "Just as every place has its acoustic signature, every listener has its own plan for hearing what it needs to."[24] What a person listening to us may need to hear is difficult to know in the best of circumstances, since frame of reference comes into play. Even so, we understand at least that sounding threatening is not what most people want to hear from us. Language is so much more than we realize until we stop to consider how we use it and then consider how the way in which we speak impacts on the hearing of others.

Give some thought to how you use language and then follow this through to examine how your characters use it. In Edward Albee's *Who's Afraid of Virginia Woolf?*, the language spoken by George is at times very arch and bordering on a kind of poetry, while at others is straight-out street language. Both of the idioms he chooses are intended as weapons, both defensive and offensive, thus giving us a lot of insight into his mental processes. In works by Len Jenkin and Suzan-Lori Parks, among others, we encounter very different uses of language shaped by an array of influences; this is echoed by some of the most gifted crafters of film dialogue: Richard Linklater, Quentin Tarantino, Miranda July and Jane Campion.

Keep in mind as you play with this etude that how a character speaks is based on everything I've discussed so far combined with the circumstances of speaking: Are they in jeopardy, relaxed, or being seductive? What are the stakes for speaking—and hearing—in a given moment? In the Coen brothers film *Miller's Crossing*, John Turturro's character Bernie says to Tom (Gabriel Byrne), "Look into your heart" several times when Tom has been sent to kill him. When he really hears Bernie, Tom relents. These are high stakes: life and death. The more you take note of the tiny variables within any context the stronger your dialogue will be.

On the hearing side of this etude the issue is how well does your character listen to the language of other people? Do they really pay attention or are they like most of us, preparing their answer while only half listening to the other? In the Buddhist tradition, listening is considered an act of compassion, of giving up one's agenda for that of the other.

As you investigate, it will be exceptionally helpful to consider a multitude of factors about your character's listening tendencies.

24. Horowitz, *The Universal Sense: How Hearing Shapes the Mind*, 47.

Auditory

Men and women listen differently to their own gender and to the opposite sex, depending on the nature of their relationship. Children listen in a limited fashion. People who have language differences encounter a lot of disconnection at times. When I tutored ESL, one of the first questions I asked a student was, "What language do you think in?" It made a difference if they were in a constant state of translating, if only to help me remember to slow down when I talked to them.

It is important to remember that a character cannot perform a negative action. "To not listen" must be realized by making it clear that the character is opting to hear anything besides what's happening at the moment: a song in their mind, the sound of passing cars.

Another aspect to pursue in the realm of hearing is the issue of relative subjectivity in the listener, based on context but also on their psychological makeup. What the receiver in a conversation may be doing in some instances is projecting onto the speaker and thus not truly hearing. Projection is a form of defense mechanism in which someone imputes thoughts, feelings, and ideas they think of as undesirable onto someone else. We do this all the time without realizing it. Someone who believes they have less power than another person might enter a conversation already feeling defensive and even combative, just because of anticipating a bad outcome.

Cultural awareness is also critical. How does your character see themselves in terms of their status in daily life? In his book *Impro*, Keith Johnstone devotes an entire chapter to improvisations that are based on perceptions of class. This evolves out of his experiences as a British subject. We Americans tend to think of ourselves as classless but that's changing as the awareness of the disparity between the very rich one percent and the rest of us becomes more manifest. Where does your character fall on the social order scale? Are they rising, falling or static? Given that, how do they listen? In film and theatre we sometimes succumb to painting characters with one color, so a very rich person is just supercilious and not listening, a poor person is a hick and incapable of understanding what's being said. This is absurd, of course, but how carefully have we explored any of our characters, not to mention ourselves, when it comes to listening or communicating?

A great approach to the listening aspect is to do a transcription of an interview or conversation. What you will discover quickly is that very few people speak in a grammatical way. We interrupt ourselves in mid-sentence, go on without any kind of pause for long sequences of words, and often don't even finish a thought. The act of carrying words from the air onto the screen or page can be tedious, but well worth the time and effort.

Another variant is what I call "Found Dialogue" in *Playwriting in Process*: i.e., eavesdropping. If you're quick enough to jot down what you're hearing, you'll find a lot of interesting stuff about how people communicate. It's especially helpful to place yourself in environments where there are a variety of backgrounds and speech patterns.

Aging has an impact on hearing that's worth an investigation, of course. Everyone loses a bit of acuity as time goes on; how do they react to that? The legendary story about Beethoven's deafness often has people perplexed: How could he hear what he wrote? The answer is that he did it like all composers do—in his mind. Yet, we understand how dismaying it must have been to him not to be able to hear his compositions in performance. The other side of this particular coin is the impact of hearing loss at any age.

Two different approaches to this etude are the use of animal voices and gibberish. Animal voices are an aspect of our global cultural heritage, thanks to Disney and Saturday morning cartoons (and all the other cartoons one can access). A Hungarian friend is a translator for television in Hungary. When she told me she did translations for cartoons my mind started to ping-pong with the possibilities. I asked her what the hardest part was, since dialogue is dialogue, and she said it was naming the characters, such as Bugs Bunny, which couldn't be translated literally and make sense. Turns out that Bugs Bunny in Hungarian is something like "Hopsy-shopsy." Hilarious. And it is as natural as anything else in the cartoon world.

To play with this variation, you can go in several directions. One is to simply imagine a character as a cartoon animal and see what happens to the way in which the now-animal speaks. In the cartoon world characters don't necessarily speak like actual people; there's a degree of exaggeration. If you work with a character as a cartoon animal it will free you from having them speak in a way that is mundane or tonally flat. Always keep in mind that you are

Auditory

taking your work into new dimensions in order to come back to where you began, better informed and more open.

The gibberish etude variation is something used in actor training all the time. Actors are asked to perform a scene using only numbers or letters of the alphabet or nonsense sounds, in order to get at the emotional core of the sequence without being hindered by any attachment to words. For an actor, one of the pitfalls is to memorize not just the sequence of words but also a way of presenting them. The gibberish exercise allows the actor to be liberated from staying within the preconceived delivery. This feeds directly into the language-as-rhythm variant that follows. If your scene feels flat, if the characters have drifted into self-explanation or reams of exposition, try asking yourself what they really want from each other at the highest conceivable level of stakes, then act out the scene on their behalf in gibberish. This might seem really crazy, and will likely feel that way until you just relax into it, but can provide you with ways of hearing the absolute emotional heart of what each character is pursuing.

In addition, something I preach to my students is that we all make nonsense and interjectory sounds when we speak. It can be very distracting to hear some government official being super careful about what they're saying by filling their statements with "um" every fifth word. That said, it's an interesting study to see how people fill in language with nonverbal sounds. Further, we all have language tics, saying "like" or "you know" in our sentences. Certainly using this in a character can be very useful.

A last variation is language-as-rhythm and how we hear that. Some of my students talk at such a rapid pace I sometimes can't follow what they're saying. The speed at which someone communicates is very much a matter of personality and culture. The same is true with hearing. It's probably as much my listening abilities as it is the high-speed delivery of the student. After all, their peers seem to follow them with no difficulty. Conversely, someone who talks very slowly can drive me to distraction. Once I realize how deliberate their delivery is, I tend to tune in and out. We all need to investigate our listening and focus habits.

Speaking and hearing are our primary modes of continuing to grow and mature. The further you dig into the ways in which your characters focus on these two aspects of our senses, the better.

Chapter Three
Sound Job Etude

In Francis Ford Coppola's film *The Conversation*, the story revolves around the work of a man who spies on people by using a range of listening devices. It's a great examination of paranoia, deception and the unreliability of the senses.

There are a number of jobs related to sound: radio and TV announcers, technicians who set up sound equipment for bands, medical people who work with sound testing, and so on. In the film and theatre worlds there are people who specialize in effects, including live, electronic and Foley studio post-production sound designed to enrich the production experience for the audience.

What's interesting in *The Conversation* is how the main character, Harry Caul, played by Gene Hackman, seems incapable of listening to what people right in front of him are saying. He hears what he wishes to as part of his job, not what is actual in exchanges with people. His last name is a great metaphorical choice, in that a caul is a harmless membrane occasionally found covering the head of a newborn baby. Harry is so closed off to the humans with whom he interacts it seems as if such a membrane was never removed.

The Conversation is a film that is built on technological know-how. There are a variety of devices for listening, recording, watching, replaying and, ultimately, for "cleaning" the sound of what had been recorded at a key moment so that the true meaning of a particular conversation comes through. Brian DePalma's film *Blow Out* uses the work of a movie sound technician as a hook into the story.

There have been a smattering of other plays, films and TV shows about people for whom sound is a key element of their world. *Talk Radio* by Eric Bogosian is about the last days of a Cleveland "shock-jock." The Terry Gilliam film *The Fisher King* centers on a similar character. David Mamet's play *The Water Engine* uses a radio broadcast in the 1930s as its setting; the play began as a radio drama, in fact. Woody Allen's *Radio Days* centers on the broadcast of Orson Welles' radio production of *War of the Worlds* that terrified a number of people.

Any job or avocation that involves very particular talents and focus can be an intriguing exploration into a character. Perhaps the character did something with sound in an early part of their life, monitoring suspected terrorist phone calls for the government or something far less sinister. This would have given the character an aural acuity that might not be needed any longer and yet plays a part in their current life. There are many ways to go with the notion of someone having had a job related to sound.

Six Degrees ...

A variation on this etude is to get some experience with writing radio drama. Writing for a medium in which sound is exclusively the means of storytelling is quite a challenge. England, Europe and other parts of the world still enjoy radio drama on a regular basis. There aren't very many outlets for radio writing in the United States, though the popularity of such National Public Radio–aired shows or podcasts as "This American Life," "Serial" and "Snap Judgment" have kept listeners involved in an aural form of storytelling over the years. For drama and comedy, the choices are limited but check out such resources as the National Audio Theatre Festival, ACB radio (produced by the American Council of the Blind) and the Sirius XM Book Radio channel from Sirius XM Satellite Radio. Depending on where you live, local radio stations occasionally produce work by residents; it might be worth your while to approach a small station with such an idea.

Of course, you don't need to have your work broadcast in order to write radio drama or comedy. The challenge of creating such work is to focus exclusively on sound and particularly to come up with locales in which sound is a major element. I've written several radio dramas that have been produced. One was set in a music store with practice and instruction rooms, another was futuristic with lots of emphasis on rocket sounds and sonic implants. It was great fun to work on these pieces as a way of digging into aural landscapes.

Although there is a limit to the kinds of actual jobs that are centered on sound in some way, keep in mind that none of us know what the future holds. Ten years ago there was no iPhone or iPad or the like; what might be the next technological advance to bring sound into our lives?

Fade Out

This will be an etude you can do over and over: it's about focused listening. All it requires is one or more willing collaborators, including your own characters.

The exercise is this: ask someone how they hear, how they listen, how hearing impacts on their life. You can base it on anything you wish, shifting as you go to other aspects, just to see where things take you and your partner in the exercise.

You might start with the most common hearing experience: music. This is not merely discussing musical tastes, though that must inevitably be part of the conversation, but can focus as well on the actual way in which the other person listens and what they listen for when they encounter music. For instance, I'm more oriented toward the instrumental aspect, melody and beat, than the lyrics. If I know all the lyrics to songs by the Beatles or Stones, it's because I've listened to their tunes hundreds of times and the lyrics sort of snuck in and got embedded. Other people tune in more quickly to the words and thus experience a given song quite differently from me. Still others only regard music as background noise.

I know people who are jazz devotees and parse every song they listen to at a level that amazes me. They can tell you what the bass player is doing at a given moment, as well as every other instrument. They know things like unique time signatures, alternate takes and the name of the producer. I love listening to them talk about this kind of stuff. The same goes for people who know a great deal about classical music or any other form. This can be done without being person to person. The radio station WWOZ in New Orleans, featured in the HBO series "Treme," is available in an online streaming format. The DJs are great appreciators of the incredible range of Louisiana-based music and give that quality of love to their broadcasts. There are also a great many podcasts about music in all forms and dimensions to check out as well. And while we're on this aspect, do you challenge yourself to listen to radio or podcasts that are atypical for you? Many of my students don't listen to National Pubic Radio, for example, and yet there are stories every day that can excite the creative mind. Listening to the news can be a drag, no doubt, but NPR has archives of their broadcasts, as well as podcasts; all well worth checking out.

Auditory 83

To return to the start: a simple way to begin this etude is to talk with some friends or associates who are music fans. After you see what evolves from those conversations, move into different areas about listening beyond the obvious. Possibilities can include discussing what or how the other person hears, in a general fashion. For example, I know someone who can isolate almost any conversation in a crowded room and listen in, as if they were a spy microphone.

Some people are especially attracted to certain kinds of voices, like those of Barry White–type basso males or the whispery Marilyn Monroe type. Others have a hard time discerning what people with unfamiliar accents are saying, regardless of the vocal pitch. Women seem—this is a generalization and like all generalizations subject to rebuttal, so forgive me—to like to talk more than men do, and they talk differently than men do. If you're male and can get permission to sit and listen while a group of women talk to each other, you will learn a very great deal. The converse would also be true for a woman to listen to a group of men talking together. I co-created a show called *Terra Incognita: Monologues and Songs About Women, Normal and Otherwise* for which a colleague, Ashley Bellet, and I had written the spoken pieces. But I also wanted to write songs for the company—all fine singers—based on their life experiences. I asked if the women would allow me to record them talking about their lives. They did and it was amazing. No punches were pulled, no self-censorship occurred; it gave me enough source material to write more than a half-dozen songs based on their conversation.

An extension of this variation is to learn how to listen to music by writing lyrics and working with a musician to create a song. It will teach you great lessons about rhythm and rhyme. A different approach is to find instrumental music that you don't know and try putting lyrics to the tune. I've used the Beatles' tune "Flying" for this and the opening whistled portion of Billy Joel's "The Stranger" as exercises in my classes.

To return to listening in our everyday experience, a more difficult approach is between intimate partners. How we hear each other in a relationship can be very tricky stuff. This can become easier when we tell each other what happens when we listen. If you're willing to take the chance, it can be very enlightening (or you could end up with separate lawyers, but let's be optimistic).

However you go about this, the main point is that it's typical for someone to assume that everyone else has the same kinds of sense experiences they do, but of course they don't. Asking someone else how they listen, what they hear when they listen, how they interact with listening and how they act upon what they've heard can be a journey as fascinating as a trip to the moon.

Applying this kind of research to a story or character will emphatically deepen your work because your awareness has itself been intensified.

This Fade Out can be applied across the board in the senses. Talking to someone else about how food tastes to them, how specific kinds of touch impacts on them, etc., can open dozens of previously hidden or unnoticed doors.

★ ★ ★

At the start of this Fade Out, I mentioned listening to your characters. In the way that life often provides interesting crosscurrents, it happens that as I'm working on the end of this chapter I'm at the 2014 Austin Film Festival. Today I attended several talks by writers and heard a great comment to share with you.

The person being interviewed in one session was Jenny Lumet, scriptwriter of *Rachel Getting Married*. Throughout the conversation Lumet returned to how she approached the various characters and their specific flaws while keeping them fully dimensional. At the end of the session Q&A, someone asked: "How were you able to write the characters in such a balanced way?"

After a thoughtful pause, Lumet said: "I listened very deeply to them."

Many writers will tell you that their characters talk to them once they've been working with the characters and story for a while. The characters seem to want to write themselves. Whether you buy into this or not, it's certainly well worth your time to consider the possibilities of listening to them, of granting them their humanity and being willing to understand even the most difficult personalities without judgment.

This can easily start by working on your listening skills, becoming more aware of how you focus your hearing, how others listen, how your characters want to be heard and so on. *Listening Is an Act of Love* is a book by David Isay, founder of StoryCorps, and the title of an animated show on PBS based on the work of StoryCorps. There's a huge archive of material from StoryCorps that's worth spending some time with, especially with regard to how people tell each other their stories: http://storycorps.org/about/archive-partners. However you define it, opening up your ears to the wealth of what there is to hear will impact on your writing in a variety of ways that may very likely surprise you.

CHAPTER FOUR

Touch
It's All Around Us

"Touch a scientist and you touch a child."
—Ray Bradbury, author

"Love consists in this, that two solitudes protect and touch and greet each other."
—Rainer Maria Rilke, author

"Reality is the leading cause of stress among those in touch with it."[25]
—Lily Tomlin, performer

As you have probably noted, there are more quotes at the start of this chapter than any other. This is because of the phenomenal range of meanings that the word "touch" has.

Diane Ackerman observes, "Our skin is what stands between us and the world."[25] It is also what connects us to the world. As you will discover in the closing chapter of the book, I break touch down into four discreet segments: tactile, the sense of surface and texture; thermal, the sense of heat and cold; kinetic, the sense of motion, even while at rest; and kinesthetic, the sense of tension or relaxation, which can also be translated as how comfortable one is in their body. I'm not being strict with these terms, in that kinesthetic and kinetic overlap: both involve motion. But someone with a kinetic awareness of not being in motion—sitting somewhere—may still

---

25. Ackerman, *A Natural History of the Senses*, 68.

have a very strong kinesthetic sense of body movement due to anxiety and tension, for example, someone with a deep fear of flying waiting in an airport to board the plane.

Touch occupies so much of our lives it's virtually impossible for us to imagine not experiencing it. As I write this sentence, my head itches a bit so I'm aware of my body transmitting a touch from within its astounding system of nerves and sensors. Immediately I scratch the itch and so now I've touched myself, and then go back to touching this keyboard. Meanwhile, I'm sensing the general temperature in my apartment (cozy on this chilly day) and simultaneously aware of the fact that my feet are not altogether happy in their slippers, but the floor is chilly so they'll just have to put up with it for a while longer. If I take the tiniest moment I can sense a host of other things: the fabric of my clothes, the feel of my tongue in my mouth, the way in which my back is aching slightly from lifting something rather heavy yesterday—all these sensations are happening in a persistently rolling tide with no need for me to do anything else except occupy space.

Yet the experience of the body is only part of this sense. As Rilke observes, touch can simply mean that we have placed our lives adjacent to or intertwined with another in an emotional sense. It's not strictly an active physical reality but alive in us because our bodies actually react to stimuli that occur to our other senses. We are touched by the sight of a person suffering or by the image of a politician we love or detest, by the winning moment in sports; through sound we are affected by music we feel deeply (it can make us dance, clap our hands, touch the air, the floor, our partner) or a lover's laugh. Our sense of smell and taste can provoke a measurable reaction in our bodies as pleasure or revulsion occurs.

The quotes from Bradbury and Rilke remind us that touching another person, whether physically or simply across the innate divide between humans, can have an extraordinary range of meanings and intentions. The feel of a baby's fingers reflexively wrapping around an offered finger, our kiss on the forehead of an ill parent, a handshake, and the infinite possibilities of touch in an intimate relationship all convey countless sensations. Touching, being touched is happening incessantly, day and night.

How we work with touch in our script process is limitless. We can certainly observe it readily in such obvious contexts as William

Gibson's play and subsequent film *The Miracle Worker*, where Helen Keller lives in a world ruled largely by feral touch until the connection between the feel of water and the word "water" spelled in her hand is made for her by Annie Sullivan. In film, there are a number of examples, including the film *Wild*. The film opens with Reese Witherspoon's character, Cheryl Strayed (author of the brilliant memoir on which the film is based), stopping atop a high promontory to deal with extremely painful feet caused by ill-fitting hiking shoes. She is forced to deal with a damaged, bloodied toenail, pulling it off. The loud and squeamish groans from the audience were proof that we immediately felt what we saw, even though we knew it was courtesy of the special effects department.

Love stories of all kinds involve touch, of course. We can enjoy the sight of someone caressing another. We cringe from abusive touch or touch that involves a kind of horror we wouldn't want to face, such as what the character Ree (Jennifer Lawrence) in *Winter's Bone* must endure, both in the form of a beating and in what she must undertake in order to finally solve her family's dilemma. Battles, ranging from Shakespearean sword fights to the pervasive modern-day depictions of war and every imaginable level of violence push our sensitivities to the limit. The highly creative approach to fighting represented by modern martial arts films, such as *Crouching Tiger, Hidden Dragon*, or the vastly more graphic Indonesian film *The Raid: Redemption*, provide an uncountable number of ways in which one human may contact another in order to defeat them.

The Greeks, of course, shied away from the kind of graphic demonstrations that later theatre undertook, but the experience of Oedipus striking out his eyes or the women of *The Bacchae* slaughtering animals—and the protagonist—is profoundly visceral even if merely described.

It's highly likely that you write elements of touch into your scripts. The question, as always, is how consciously do you use this sense in your writing?

The etudes that follow will provide you with a range of explorations in this sense. You can certainly start from paying attention in this moment to touch: observing how you're holding this book or electronic device, where you are in space, what your clothes feel like on your body and so on.

Before you begin imagining and writing, I want to recommend an exercise that you'll find intriguing. It's based on an exercise by Viola Spolin called Begin/End. You can see a demonstration of one approach to this at http://www.spolingamesonline.org/portfolio-items/begin-end/. The instructor is demonstrating how to work with invisible objects as part of acting training.

My version is to work with actual objects, such as picking up a pencil or pen to write with it. If you break down the movements into their tiniest segments, you'll find that before your hand grips the object there is a begin/end movement of your hand from resting place to reach the object. You might even consider the act of lifting your hand from your lap, for instance, as a begin, then counting the point before you start the downward reach as an end. It all depends on how minutely you want break down the exercise. If you get really super strict about this you'll find that the tiniest movements are begin/end. Begin: your hand moves to the object; end: it stops near the object; begin: your hand turns to be in the correct position to pick up the object; end: your hand is now in position; begin: your fingers close to grip the object; end: they grip it—and so on. If you carry this through to the action of writing with the pen or pencil, you will see that the actuality of touch in what we consider a simple, mundane action is actually extremely complex.

If you then add each awareness of touch just in the room (notice the temperature; notice the texture of the paper you'll write on) as a begin/end you'll have a much greater awareness of the way in which touch is incessantly transmitting information to our brains and nervous systems. Finally, if you're having a day when you seem to be exceptionally clumsy, turning your activities into a begin/end exercise might just save you from dropping that glass.

Key Etude: Temperature

It's a long-running joke that one thing sure to tax a relationship is who gets to control the thermostat in the dwelling place or the car.

In this etude, your exploration is into the way in which a character experiences temperature in a variety of circumstances. As a start, consider writing scenes in which the heat or cold is at an extreme. In *Star Wars V: The Empire Strikes Back*, Luke nearly dies in the subarctic temperatures of the icy planet Hoth. In the play *K2*, by Patrick Meyers, two climbers are stranded on a ledge to which they've fallen, trying to conquer the mountain. In the neo-noir film *Body Heat*, the characters collude and collide in the midst of a Florida heat wave. Tennessee Williams had an affinity for plays set in hot locales, such as *A Streetcar Named Desire* and *Night of the Iguana*, or heat references, with titles such as *Suddenly, Last Summer* and *Summer and Smoke*.

As a starting point, try tracking your character through the seasons, if the world of the play is where clear seasons exist. I'm one of those people who love autumn, truly reveling in it; a friend once floored me when she said, "In autumn, I grieve," referring to the end of warmth and greenery. How does your character react to the autumn leaves, or cope with a very hot and muggy summer as opposed to a severe winter? Do they have enough awareness to prepare for the seasons in terms of their clothing and home space? Or does vanity or immaturity get the best of them and they go out into the cold poorly dressed? Is your character someone who likes to slowly roast in the sun on a towel or do they shun the outdoors entirely in hot weather? Are they someone who tans easily or burns? If you've never had a severe sunburn or frostbite, count yourself lucky. How would your character cope with either circumstance?

Examine the way in which the day itself affects your character, regardless of season. Some people have a lot of difficulty coping with gray days; others take them in stride. Many who live in big cities have to cope with the weather on a daily basis as they commute from home to work or school; it's very rare that a subway platform in New York, for instance, isn't steamy or frigid; the shelters that are provided at bus stops are absurdly inadequate. How might your character navigate a range of temperatures in a new environment? One person could easily pass through a range of climates just going from apartment to work: home might be at an ideal temperature, the car heater might not work so well or the bus/train is overheated, the outside temperature is too high or too low, and then the office's thermal environment is extreme.

Temperature is also an internal matter. Some people run below or above the 98.6 degrees considered normal. This has an impact on how the person feels overall. A below normal body temperature can be an indicator of a variety of maladies, such as diabetes,

Addison's disease and even shock. Above normal is indicative of fever, which might be accompanied by sweating and dizziness or worse, depending on the degrees above 98.6. It might be very interesting to look at how your character would live their life if being affected by any of these problems, whether as a persistent or emergency state. What if your character is someone who has an exceptionally low or high average temperature, yet functions just fine? How does this affect their world and choices?

Six Degrees . . .

Interior temperature is also a factor in how a person experiences the world. When I taught public speaking it was normal to see a student blush or start to flush as they stood before the class. In some cases it would be severe and I would worry about whether the speaker was going to need medical help. There is a condition called rosacea, which can manifest as a persistently red face or as facial burning, a swollen nose or symptoms in the eyes. Whether the character is affected by a condition that requires medical attention or simply has anxiety issues or skin that naturally shows reddishness when they feel uncomfortable, there's a lot of potential in exploring how this affects their life. Perhaps there are plots to explore as well. There was an episode in season two of the TV show "Grey's Anatomy" involving a character with extreme blushing, for instance; her condition was painful and often led people to make many wrong assumptions about her.

Temperature is an element of our intimate lives. In moments of sexual intimacy, we are functioning at a higher temperature. In a state of contented cuddling, we share our warmth with our partner or child. A baby loves being swaddled for warmth and security. Explore the various situations in which your character would seek out comfort through warmth. In comparison, how would they react to being next to someone who was too warm? What is your character's comfort level in terms of another's body warmth or cold; how might their reactions create circumstances that are either ideal or problematic? What would their reaction be to someone whose body was warm but had feet like blocks of ice? You can riff on this in many different ways, keeping in mind that any work you do does not have to be limited to a particular genre. Sure, icy feet can be funny but what if the feet belong to a person who has started to die from the ground up?

In severe temperatures people sometimes take their entire family into the bed to keep everyone warm, even adding domestic animals. The band named Three Dog Night got its moniker apparently from Australian Aborigines, who slept surrounded by their animals in the coldest weather. In the *Star Wars V* episode, Han Solo slices open the belly of the tauntaun to save Luke from freezing to death. Tough on the tauntaun, but, well, the Force had to continue somehow. What would your character do in order to avoid freezing to death or dying from the heat? Punishment for prisoners can occasionally involve temperature. In the film *Bridge on the River Kwai*, the punishment for any infraction is to be placed in a closed hut or, worse, an iron box in the tropical heat. In the film *One Day in the Life of Ivan Denisovitch*, based on the novel by Aleksandr Solzhenitsyn, the title character is forced to spend the night in an unheated cell with no bedclothes in a gulag prison where the temperatures average well below zero.

Finally, temperature and humidity are functions of geography. Clearly, one would have an interesting personality to explore in a character who wants to live in the Arctic Circle or Antarctica, or who opts for the extreme elements found in Africa. I was totally unprepared for the incessant heat and humidity of Singapore, which averages around 80 degrees daily, as opposed to happily surprised by the exceptionally pleasant dry climate of Aruba, which also averages roughly 80 degrees, but is cooled and dehumidified by the trade winds. This readily lends itself to the kind of plot where an outsider penetrates an unfamiliar or unknown culture. The film *Avatar* is based on this notion, as are any number of other films.

You can learn a lot from your own experiences with temperatures of all kinds and by observing others. Some people never seem to be content, no matter the temperature, while others are stoic about it and still others seem to take little note either way. Certainly it's one of the most common topics of conversation we experience, whether it's someone complaining about the heat or reveling in a bright spring day. The joke, especially where the climate is highly changeable, goes: "if you don't like the weather, wait a minute."

Hands Etude

This etude may be the most obvious one for touch. It will encompass a great many areas. We use our hands in a wide variety of ways ranging from the simple touch to our face when nervous or itchy to creating complex master works with food, visual art or music—to performing lifesaving surgery.

The first exploration for you to consider is having a look at the way in which you use your hands for various activities, compared to observing how other people use theirs, and applying what you notice to a given character. For instance, some people have shaky hands. Perhaps an illness has affected them or it's just a natural state. Others have hands that are admirable for their photogenic quality. Some people have hands that are clumsy, others that are deft. This exploration might work best for a situation where you already know the plot so that you can examine how the character's hands function in context. It could also be useful to be aware of what they do for a living and how that may manifest in their hands. Are they calloused from doing carpentry or working with animals? Are they soft and refined looking, with a manicure? Are they missing a finger or part of one? How did that happen and what impact does it have on the character?

Perhaps your character's hands have a sort of life of their own. In the book and film of *The Day of the Locust*, the main character, Tod Hackett, has overly large hands and is constantly making shapes with them. The hands of Robert DeNiro's character in *Raging Bull* are powerful weapons, in and out of the boxing ring, and then symbols of his broken dreams after he batters them against a jail cell wall.

Six Degrees . . .

There are so many jobs in which the use of the hands is critical, ranging from a chef to an astronaut working in space. You might find that a character's backstory about how they once used their hands could be very informative. Certainly someone who had been in the military and who had used their hands for wounding and killing or for dealing with dangerous materials might use their hands in the present day in a very careful or circumspect way. This would likely be an unconscious matter for them and intriguing for you to create. A former musician might fall into a reverie state and discover their hands shaping chords or exercising fingering patterns. How might you use this to your advantage in your script? Could this be something as simple as a clue about their past or might it be more nuanced and reveal a personality aspect of some sort? Our hands seem to remember things for us, such as where the ignition is in the car or just how high to reach for a glass in a cabinet when we're not even looking or the feel of an infant's downy head. What memories might the hands of your character have that could reveal aspects about them? When Sweeney Todd gets his razors back he proclaims that his arm is complete again. What rediscovered items or situations would provide your character's hands with a sense of completeness?

In the character's present world, what skills might they have that can enhance their story for you? People who can juggle, play difficult instruments (like a sitar or mandolin) or do card tricks all have specific kinds of hand skills. Those who can knit, sew or make a quilt, or anything domestic have a different set of abilities. I had an acquaintance who worked out her occasional depressions by spending a whole day making numerous loaves of bread from scratch by hand. Certain people I've observed seem to have a hard time doing nothing. You can see them in an incessant state of activity, making food, fixing household appliances, sorting clothes to give away, cleaning, reorganizing, making scrapbooks and so on. What drives that person's activities—are the movements of their hands a kind of language?

This opens several other aspects about hands to consider: sign language, hand gestures, and how hands are used in performance circumstances, such as music and spoken word.

A certain percentage of students opt for sign language in order to fulfill a university's language requirement. Some do so for altruistic reasons, wanting to be interpreters or to communicate with a specific individual. Some choose this route rather than having to take the foreign languages they find difficult to learn. From my point of view as a hearing person and artist, sign language is not merely a physical translation of sound but a kind of dance. It's also fun to watch someone signing who is using a slang version of the standard American Sign Language because the body is often much more animated. A character who uses sign language for particular purposes has a relationship with their hands quite unique from that of people who do not sign. If they are a hearing person, how does signing impact on their use of spoken language?

It's a commonplace cliché that certain ethnic groups use their hands more than others. This may bear out in certain instances but all people use their hands to one degree or another for making themselves clear. We illustrate what we're talking about. I've always been amused watching people talk on a phone and gesticulate as they do so. There's no one to see them unless they're using a video feature, so why should the hands be used? Gestures provide emphasis, underscoring, sometimes even a kind of counterpoint or rhythmic underscore to what we're saying. If for no other purpose, many of us—possibly most—have utilized certain gestures while driving, usually offering wordless advice to another driver as to their skills or manners. How does your character use their hands in terms of gestures? It can be interesting to annotate gestures in one's script, while staying open to what an actor will bring to the meaning of the gesture through the dynamic of their body.

There's a term in acting, "the psychological gesture," which at the basic level means the way in which the body expresses what's going on in the mind. The concept comes from master acting teacher Michael Chekhov, who developed it back in the 1930s. You can find a lot of information about it online (the primary site is http://chekhov.net/index.htm) and in books, so I won't go into it too far except to cite one example. When I saw *Long Day's Journey into Night* on Broadway in 2003, I was intrigued by what Philip Seymour Hoffman did with his physicalization of the woebegone James "Jamie" Tyrone, Jr. As his character sank further into despair and alcoholism, Hoffman began to shield his eyes as someone might from the sun. It began as a kind of nervous touching of his forehead and by Act IV had turned into a virtual covering of his eyes, as if to prevent anyone from truly seeing him. It was a very effective choice.

We all have nuances of our physical expression that we might not pay much attention to but are well worth exploring alongside observing these things in others. This can range from simple tics that speak about anxiety—clicking pens in the classroom is one I often notice—to full-blown self-touching, nail biting, incessant hair fussing and so on. These are generally physical aspects of personality that the individual might not be aware of at all. We humans are so remarkably communicative on such an array of levels!

In the performance realm, use of the hands is a fascinating study. In music, for instance, back in the 1980s, David Byrne of the Talking Heads band used deliberately unnatural gestures while performing, as a kind of alienation device: don't take all this so seriously (e.g., the message in "Stop Making Sense," the title of their soundtrack album and movie; Byrne repeats the phrase "Stop Making Sense" several times in the song entitled "Girlfriend Is Better"). A great deal of punk and new wave performance utilized gestures in ways not previously seen in rock and pop performance, perhaps influenced by the dominance of MTV videos in the era.

In recent years, the rise of slam poetry and hip-hop culture have created a style of performance that has roots in a variety of realms, such as the griot in Africa, the dub style of improvisation used by reggae DJs and the poets of the Black Power movement in the 1960s, and the oratorical style of preachers in African American churches, among others. Slam-style poets often "conduct" their rhymes or use the highly aggressive gestures one sees in rap performance. Analogous to this is watching Buddhist monks in training having loud debates over aspects of Dharma texts, such as the Heart Sutra, where the senior monk will shoot his hand toward the junior monk, making a clapping sound as a signal for the other to respond. The gestures seem almost threatening but are simply a matter of energizing the debate. Would your character have an innate reference to performance gesture in their daily activities? Certainly we all talk differently in distinct contexts, so how might the physicalization of your character vary in disparate circumstances? How difficult might they find it to drop their public persona once in private?

There are so many obvious occupations that rely on the use of the hands: sports, mechanics of all kinds, medical and dental work, people who do massage or specialized manipulation techniques, even fortune-tellers. What does your character do for a living that might impact and enhance their meaning in the story you're telling? In a play I wrote about a woman who seeks a sperm donor, the main character is driven by a profound fear that her biological clock is running out. The man she eventually meets repairs and makes watches. I wanted his awareness of time to be as great as hers, not to mention being someone who might have a delicate touch for a woman in a state of near despair.

There are a number of jobs where touch is an obvious element of personality. In some instances, touch is either an issue or an asset.

For example, might your character be someone who is prone to touch other people in social contexts? Are they "handsy," as the expression goes, ranging from a general way to an extreme of practically being a molester? If so, where did that come from in their past? I've been in situations where someone from a different culture tends to stand very close when talking; it's hard not to back away in such an instance. Close proximity is not terribly comfortable for some people, where for others it's normal. It's tricky when boundaries are transgressed but truly worthwhile to see what happens to a character in that situation—from both sides. We know that culture plays a large role in a variety of ways. I remember a friend from Iran telling me that it's not unusual to see men in Iran walking together holding hands. In most places in America that would be shocking to many people and accompanied by all manner of assumptions.

In other circumstances, touching can be an asset. Certainly someone comforting someone they don't know, a child or a very old person, is crossing a relatively soft boundary. The way in which people in certain positions make contact with our bodies is an intriguing investigation. We think nothing of a hairstylist or barber touching our heads, where if someone did it out of the blue in a diner, we'd be freaked out. Not to mention the dozens of ways in which our doctors make contact with us. There's a level of trust and willingness involved in permitting someone to move into our personal space, a vulnerability. How will your character react to a variety of ways of being touched? A general doctor's visit is no big thing; having a prostate or gynecological exam is something else altogether.

In certain professions, touching the other person is a kind of sales tactic, a way to break through resistance in a customer. We don't think about the way in which a shoe salesperson might touch our feet or the manner in which someone glad-hands us in a variety of contexts. People who serve the public develop ways of making an additional level of communication. For example, Diane Ackerman cites the following: "In a[n] . . . experiment in Oxford, Mississippi, waitresses lightly and unobtrusively touch diners on the hand or shoulder. Those customers who are touched don't necessarily rate the food or the restaurant better, but they consistently tip the waitress higher."[26] If you keep yourself from limiting the possible

---

26. Ibid., 123.

jobs your character might have or have had, you might open any number of doors on their sense of making contact with others. To avoid being literal, stay loose to the idea that there's all kinds of contact, even in the way someone uses their voice when they do their job, sounding ultra confident or speaking in such a knowing way you feel they're a friend. Your character might just have a naturally warm personality or they may have the instincts and feather touch of a pickpocket.

Intimate Touch Etude

I'm not going to get graphic or detailed here. This etude is about various kinds of intimacy and the nature of touch in those circumstances. Making a very open investigation of the nature of intimate touch could be very beneficial to your character explorations. Our social anxieties and individual interactions are deeply affected by our sense of personal space. How closely touched are we willing to be and by whom; how completely do we wish to touch another? When we explore this on behalf of a character we begin to open doors on their most guarded and unguarded natures.

To begin a little way from the subject that might be difficult for some, we can start with the relatively simple pleasure of cuddling with a loved one or providing loving touch, ranging from a child to a dear friend to a dying relative. Our first intimacy is with our mothers, fathers or caregivers. Aspects of your character may have been greatly affected by this first state of physical contact and trust. How they behave in the present time could be greatly dependent on both positive and negative experiences from infancy on into childhood. There's a powerful moment in *Rebel Without a Cause* where Natalie Wood's character, Judy, tries to sit on her father's lap, as her little brother had just done. Her father pushes her off saying that she's too old for that; her disappointment and anger are palpable.

In adulthood, sharing warm contact with friends or providing comfort to someone who is in the hospital or hospice is part of our own ritual of moving from birth to death. The thought of touching another who has a transmittable disease is the very last thing some people would do; others take to it with relative ease. At the time of this writing, the Ebola epidemic is widespread in West

Africa. We admire the Doctors Without Borders who go to Sierra Leone, knowing we might not be able to summons such courage, but we will rush to the bedside of a child or friend without worrying much about the consequences. We know that we cannot heal them; we go in order to share our human spirit and hope. Or we do not. Where would your character fall in that spectrum? When Louis leaves Prior Walter in *Angels in America*, he denies his lover any comforting touch. His profound fear of contracting Prior Walter's HIV/AIDS drives him out of their home and relationship. We likely abhor his choice (and self-acknowledged cowardice) and yet we understand the sheer human terror behind his action.

Six Degrees . . .

This point of variation brings us to our sexuality and how we examine the sexuality of our characters. It's staggering to consider the amount of disinformation, mystification, taboo, mythology, fear and who-knows-what in modern American society when it comes to sex. As you encounter this aspect of intimacy, a wide variety of conflicting emotions, assumptions and so on may present themselves to you. Or possibly not—stay as open as you can to your ways of thinking in this regard and how great your awareness is of others. We talk about sex, we joke about it, we don't deny ourselves the opportunity to admire the physicality of another person whether on the Internet or in person. Sex is a major part of our lives. We are profoundly biological organisms with vast capabilities of comprehending what drives us and being in synch with those elements of our personality—or not. Consider the number of ways you might develop characters and circumstances in which sexuality is the primary element. How they address their needs can be extraordinarily revealing to you as they manifest in your script. Consider the variations on carnality in the film *Chinatown*, for one example, or how the subject is approached in *Spring Awakening*, both the original play by Frank Wedekind and subsequent musical adaptation.

During early adolescence, both boys and girls start to explore their sexuality. This can be expressed in a variety of ways, ranging from teasing contact (being bashed by a backpack can equate to a declaration of love) to more explicit experimentation. It's at this point in their development when a person begins to understand their desires and preferences. The experience of a first kiss can be overwhelming for some, underwhelming for others. It's the same with first everything in the early exploratory years.

You can extend this into how your character responds in sexual situations. What do they like? What do they shy away from? How well does the character know their sexuality and responsiveness? If they are a shy lover, what might change that? If they are closed off in certain ways, what caused that? What is their deepest personal history when it comes to meeting the body of another human in a sexual context?

As with all of the etudes, this can begin with paying attention to yourself in all of the circumstances where you make full contact with someone. Some people are raised in homes where there is little touching; others experience an environment of open and highly physical warmth. If you haven't given much thought to your own background and its impact on you, this is a good moment in which to do so. How did your preferences evolve as you grew up? Was it difficult to be intimate with another person? Were you into serial relationships or did you seek to be with one person for life? Where did/do you fall on the spectrum? Are you straight, gay, bi? This may be difficult stuff but it's worth taking the risk to be utterly honest with yourself. As you track your experience, you may encounter memories that are tricky or that are enlightening. Only go where you're comfortable, but pay close attention to how these things affect you—there may be absolute gold for the creation of a character. I remember a friend in New York who came out of the closet at the age of sixty. He had been married, raised kids and done the entire middle-class thing, but he knew he wasn't living truthfully. When I met him he had embraced his homosexuality, fallen in love with a very caring man and was one of the happiest people I'd ever met. How candid can your character be about their sexuality in the face of social and familial realities? What risks are they willing to take?

Sexuality is such a tricky thing for us in the West to talk about. We are still reeling from the historical impact of certain beliefs that were founded on fear, shame and prohibition rather than openness. And certainly the political terrain hasn't moved very far forward as of this writing. The worst thing we can do in any of our writing is to make assumptions on behalf of our characters. If your character is a transsexual and you aren't, you need to do the research that will give you the fullest understanding of that life experience. If your character has secret desires that you invent but don't fully grasp or fear, find a way to do the research. There isn't much that you cannot find on the Internet but don't bypass first-person research. If you find you can't write with probity, then maybe you should bail out of the script until you can. Better that than to sit there typing away at a character who is a sham. In the ultimate sense of touch, a writer needs to be as intimate with their characters as the characters are in their most private lives.

This suggests the possibility of writing monologues versus scenes, which can be an excellent approach to character development. Keep in mind that a monologue is a character arguing with themselves internally over something. The more doubt the character has, the greater level of conflict, the stronger your work will be.

Intimate touch can simply be a hug when the person being embraced has gone without physical contact for a while. A character who lives in a big urban environment can experience a level of isolation that can be soul crushing. It's not easy to be the person who lives alone (with or without cat), goes to work as an anonymous commuter, works all day without much or any personal interaction with coworkers, then returns to their apartment to spend the evening in a state of silence except for the company of some form of media. What would your character do to find some means of contact with another? In a way, this is the premise of the film *Her*, but it could also be an aspect in many other movies, ranging from the 1950s drama *Marty*, to sci-fi explorations such as *Solaris* (both the Russian original and American remake) and the British-made *Moon*, and on to realistic films such as *Midnight Cowboy* and *Jeremiah Johnson*. Samuel Beckett excelled at creating characters living in dreadful isolation such as *Krapp's Last Tape* and *Happy Days* (not to be confused with the TV show).

People sometimes feel the intrusive presence of another on subways or buses. This is caused by overcrowding but may also be behavior on the part of a person with molester tendencies—and yet, might it be the unconscious need of a deeply lonely person for any form of contact? Not to excuse, but merely to wonder at the limitlessness of human despair. If you place your character in a state of profound isolation, how will they behave? What kinds of choices might they make? How innately social are they? What do they lack in their lives that they can't seem to solve except through aberrant behavior?

There's also the question of what kind of hugger your character might be. Are they someone who grabs another in a bear-like smother or who gives either a side hug or clavicle touch? In Paula Vogel's *How I Learned to Drive*, L'il Bit tries to avoid slow dancing with the boys, hyper-aware and greatly embarrassed by having large breasts. You can expand this as an exploration to even the simple act of shaking hands. Some people extend what amounts to a long-dead fish while others can nearly break your hand. Politicians love the two-hander: grip with the right and place the left on top. There are wonderful variants on the handshake, sometimes amounting to a thirty-second ritual.

Ultimately, the nature of intimate touch is determined by an uncountable number of factors. How we touch, why we touch, how we feel about being touched and by whom, and how intimately, are all fantastic elements to explore in the psyche of your characters.

Touch as Self Etude

Diane Ackerman: "What is a sense of one's self? To a large extent it has to do with touch, how we feel. Our *proprioceptors* (from Latin for 'one's own' receptors) keep us informed about where we are in space, if our stomachs are busy . . . where our legs, arms, head are, how we're moving, what we feel like from moment to moment."[27]

Some people can navigate well in the dark, trusting the feel of the surface they're moving over. Some have a great awareness of touch in terms of how their skin reacts to things, whether it's the ability to instantly know that a fabric is synthetic or linen, or to immediately determine on contact such things as whether something is soft, hard, heavy, light, etc.

Our sense of touch is what helps us separate who we are from others. It defines the way in which we move through the world but even more greatly, according to Ackerman: "Touch fills our

---

27. Ibid.

memory with a detailed key as to how we're shaped. A mirror would mean nothing without touch."[28]

A three-dimensional awareness of the world provides another treasure chest of etude possibilities for you. If we simply stop for a moment and consider touch on the broadest scale of selfhood we can speculate for hours on end.

Certainly our sense of self as we grow from child to adult is an ongoing process well worth exploring in a character. In Richard Linklater's *Boyhood*, we witness this very thing as Mason Evans Jr. changes from a six-year-old child to a young man of eighteen. Mason's self-awareness through his awkward early years and adolescence gives way to a person striving to be comfortable in the world.

We can benefit from spending time looking through photos and videos of ourselves, trying to reach back into our own sense of physical and mental selves in order to come to a better understanding of what a character may have experienced. Perhaps we are unconsciously calling on our own background without realizing we've meshed it with a character. It's critical to be very forgiving of ourselves when we do this and nonjudgmental. How we look in a given image is how we looked at that point; we need to be grateful to that younger version for surviving the awkwardness, pimples and so forth.

Six Degrees ...

Another approach to this etude is to look at the reality of phobias, many of which are rooted in touch: claustrophobia (fear of being trapped), haphephobia (fear of being touched), agliophobia (fear of pain), hedonophobia (fear of feeling pleasure), among others. You can have a great time exploring aspects of character through the lists of phobias found on various websites. We certainly don't want to be cruel, but some phobias are rather funny and open up avenues of backstory for a character that might be greatly useful to you: fear of garlic, fear of chins or fear of words strike me as especially provocative material. Phobias develop because of a traumatic event, witnessing another person experiencing a traumatic event, or learning about something that seems threatening or frightening.

---

28. Ibid., 95.

Most of us had falls on our bikes or skates and the like. We got up, dusted ourselves off and continued along. The person who cannot do this, who develops a lifelong fear of bicycles, is considered phobic. Coming back from these kinds of fears is very difficult, though most are treatable.

Examining the nature of a character through their phobic experience of the world can lead to many variations on how humans live and how we cope. There are obvious outlets for this in horror/thriller films like *Arachnophobia* and *Jaws*, not to mention the double-whammy phobia film *Snakes on a Plane*. Less obvious examples would be *Bonnie and Clyde*, where Clyde seems to have a fear of women or intimacy, or a related film with a comic point of view, *The 40-Year-Old Virgin*. Plays that deal with phobic circumstances include *Equus*, where a boy blinds horses because he fears they've seen him "sinning," and *The Curious Incident of the Dog in the Night-Time*, where the main character has autism spectrum disorder and will instantly lash out at anyone who touches him.

As with any etude, it's worthwhile to examine our own phobias. Most of us don't have many irrational fears, but we probably all have at least one that's always lurking and ready to get loose.

Another avenue of investigation, although one that is treated too often in a clichéd fashion, is the nature of addiction. In this instance the sense of touch is rooted in the feeling someone experiences due to alcohol, drugs, etc. As mentioned at various points previously, it's critical to do research—first-person where possible—in order to truly understand and write with candor about what the person experiences. There are too many assumptions about addicts in theatre, television and film, going all the way back to the loonily absurd *Reefer Madness* up through every other cop show. If you want to write about an addict, consider where you might begin. In addition, the possibilities of what a person may be addicted to opens up the avenues of exploration for you, if you keep the definition broad and loose enough.

A related addiction or obsession is to tattoos, piercings and body alterations such as split tongues, ear gauges and the like. So many people seem to collect tattoos to the point where very little of them is not inked. How far would your character go in this area? There are people who have full-body tattoos, for example. Ray Bradbury drew on this for his story collection entitled *The Illustrated Man*, which was adapted into a film. The other end of the spectrum is where someone has gotten a tattoo they eventually come to regret. In the realm of body alterations what would your character prefer? Would they be secret or on active display? The possibilities of what can be pierced seem pretty limitless; what would your character choose? What would your character be like if they were or had been someone who did piercing or tattooing? It's a very intimate quality of touch, even though the contact may largely be through the tattoo device. In addition, there's a very pronounced subculture one encounters in the tattoo or piercing world, where people have taken the choice to an extreme. This is something well-worth looking into for character study.

In fact, there are subcultures of subcultures in this particular world. Heather Langencamp, who played Nancy in the *Nightmare on Elm Street* films, directed a documentary called *I Am Nancy*, in which she looks at the disparity of how her character is only slightly commercialized versus that of Freddy Krueger (Robert Englund), whose image can be found in a host of forms. The film starts in a tattoo shop where someone is having the image of Freddy needled into their skin, and throughout the film others display their tattoos of the killer as well as numerous other figures from horror films. Who might your character have inked onto their body? Would it be Freddy or Daffy Duck—or Nancy?

To look at the less-extreme aspect of Touch as Self, it's worth spending time to keep an awareness of your own self as you are right now. We experience our bodies in a vast range of ways on a daily basis. We clean and feed our bodies; we clothe ourselves and add elements that are designed to help us cope with the weather. We pay attention to the details of our physical selves that change in a normal way: we cut our nails, put on lip balm and hand lotion, brush our hair. As time goes on, some of our daily ministrations change because we either need to pay more or less attention: our skin grows drier, we are less supple, we lose hair. Our physical dimensions change: we lose or gain weight, we become taller in our young days and start to shrink in later life.

Our awareness of our physical selves is a constant, but one that many pay little attention to until something brings them to recognize that they've lost muscle tone or gained another pound. Some people are much more obsessive about their bodies than others; some are utterly indifferent. How does your character interact with their body, how has that changed over time, how much or little do they worry about the changes, and how far will they go to correct what they don't like? In these days of plastic surgery and Botox, there's little that can't be remodeled, replaced, or made larger or smaller. In this instance you might look at vanity as an aspect of touch. Who we see in the mirror defines the self we wish to believe we are and we rarely see ourselves in a truthful manner.

Mobility Etude

The issue of mobility is certainly a factor in many people's lives. Things can change radically as someone copes with injury, disease or aging. Our focus in this segment is on how your character moves through the world. Some people are natural runners, some not so much. Some can dance, some can gracefully accomplish the knee and back torture known as gardening; some can barely walk down the street without tripping, bashing into something or dropping everything they're carrying. These are the kinetic and kinesthetic aspects of touch.

How your character encounters the physical planes of their life is a truly fun exploration to undertake. All of us are awkward at one point or another, of course. How and whether we overcome this can be a very telling aspect of character to examine. The way in which your character transits from the relatively fluid state of childhood through the gangly newborn pony phase of adolescence, and into the self they carry through adulthood will provide you with a wealth of considerations. This can include hypothesizing as to how they will age.

It can also include speculation on their background. In the Whit Stillman film *Metropolitan*, for example, we meet a group of young men and women who physicalize themselves as people twenty years older and from a long ago era. They affect a jadedness and languor that is reflected in their bodies except in unguarded moments. This is something one can readily write into a script as a treasure trove of possibilities for the actors and director. In the Sam Shepard play *Fool for Love* the main male character is a stuntman and rodeo competitor. His gait and posture is that of someone who has suffered many injuries and broken bones.

Six Degrees . . .

An extension of this would be to throw the character into explorations that interest you on their behalf, such as fulfilling a rigorous bucket list. How will they perform trying to climb a mountain or learning to tango? It's critical in this kind of work to be compassionate and keep in mind that you are trying to craft fully dimensional characters. We can easily be tempted to thrust our protagonist into a slapstick circumstance but what is the reality that underscores it? Yes, they may look ridiculous but what is the underlying passion that has driven them to undertake the task? In the film *Breaking Away*, in the climactic "Little 500" bike race, Cyril (Daniel Stern) leaps on his team's bicycle and looks positively absurd in doing so, too gawky and gangling for the bike. But in that moment's laughter we know that he's doing his absolute best to support his best friend, Dave, who has been injured and can't compete. We understand as well that Cyril has a history of failing yet somehow remains undaunted and jumps in to help without hesitation.

What is your character's sense of self through movement? How do they cope with whatever may make movement an issue, whether it be from innate incoordination or because of physical inability in some form? Are they capable of breaking into free-form dance like Greta Gerwig's character in *Frances Ha* or are they doomed to a life of klutzy bungling like the protagonist of *Napoleon Dynamite*?

Selfhood is a lifelong process of discovery, effort and acceptance when it works; when it doesn't it can be a slow descent into disappointment or at least a state of complacency. How your character copes with this process through their physical self-awareness, self-love or self-loathing will be profoundly effective for your explorations.

Pain Etude

Wellness is certainly a huge aspect of touch—we like to feel at ease in our bodies. When we don't, when pain shows up, a great many things change.

For the purpose of this etude I'm going to lump in such seemingly unrelated things such as ticklishness, cultural practices in which pain is an element and a little bit about emotional pain.

Pain is an aspect of touch that can be immediate, almost to the same degree that smell is to the brain. When we experience sudden pain, the nerves send an instantaneous message right to the spinal cord, causing a reflex. The pain can come in the form of touching something too hot or very sharp; it can also be a flinch response to a loud sound or sudden burst of light.

A lot of people live with perpetual pain. It can range from something internal like acid reflux or physical distress that reaches a level of ten on a ten-point scale. It's impossible to get through life without experiencing some form of pain or another, but for a person in constant pain the way that they live is very much dictated by the presence of this nagging discomfort. People who have been injured in automobile accidents have recurring back or neck issues. Military or law enforcement personnel suffer horrendous injuries that never leave their bodies or their minds.

For example you might create a history of pain that will open up a character's personality to deepen them for you and for an audience. You can examine it from a variety of perspectives including how well they tolerate the pain, if they self-medicate or whether the pain is actual. We have Laura from *The Glass Menagerie* as an example of this. Williams suggests that Laura's limp might be more a matter of mental reality than physical, but leaves it open as to whether she suffers or not.

Pain may not be the result of a trauma; it is occasionally the result of birth defects or DNA. A revival of the play *The Elephant Man* is in previews on Broadway at the time of this writing. This is a character whose life is entirely centered on physical and psychological torment. It is also a characterization that places a good deal of physical stress on the performer, since the condition of Joseph Merrick can only be suggested on stage by an actor contorting himself. In the David Lynch film, makeup prostheses recreate the actual look of the character but it's no less demanding on an actor to labor under hot lights wearing pounds of latex.

You may not want to rewrite an Elephant Man character, of course, but it's worth your time to consider what would constitute anything resemblant in a character. A friend had terrible foot problems requiring surgery that was extremely painful to recover from and which has never been fully alleviated. This was a problem that had developed during adolescence. What would your character be like if they were in a state of persistent embarrassment due to a condition they could not easily correct? Or in a state of pain that prevented them from being able to concentrate on tasks or join in the social world around them? How might these early experiences manifest in the present or in the future?

Analogous to this is the degree of pain that a person can or cannot tolerate. It's been said that women have a higher pain threshold than men. This is imperative, given how arduous and body-altering giving birth is. How someone experiences pain is both a physical and a mental reality. Some individuals are capable of ignoring or "playing through" pain, as it is often called in the world of sports. Others can be brought to their knees by a hangnail. Maria Irene Fornes has the character Orlando, a military torturer, describe this in a rather offhanded fashion in her play *The Conduct of Life*: "Some people get a cut in a finger and die. Because their veins are right next to their skin. There are people who, if you punch them in the stomach the skin around the stomach bursts and the bowels fall out. Other people, you cut them open and you don't see any veins. You can't find their intestines. There are people who don't even bleed."[29] As disturbing as this speech is, what's remarkable is how nonchalant Orlando is about what he's describing and what he does for a living. One wonders at *his* ability to feel pain.

Perhaps the greatest challenge in the world of scriptwriting is exemplifying pain in a way that isn't gratuitous or merely appealing to the lowest common denominator. It seems that when a form of pain is shown happening to an aspect of the human body that we feel protective of, such as the damaged toenail in *Wild* or the fingernails of George Clooney's character in *Syriana*, we have a visceral reaction. When it's people beating the living hell out of each other, we don't really feel at a very deep level unless the film has generated a sense of empathy. The stage is less a place of overt violence than film, yet there are examples of disturbing scripts such as *The Pillow Man, Blasted* and *The Sport of My Mad Mother*, as well as some plays by Sam Shepard and Tracy Letts, among others.

---

29. Fornes, Maria Irene. *Maria Irene Fornes: Plays.* (Cambridge, MA: PAJ Plays, MIT Press, 2001), 79.

Six Degrees . . .

As you develop a given character, there are a great many ways in which you can explore them through the matter of pain. Certainly examining how someone deals with pain is the immediate choice, but what about someone who either enjoys giving pain or is forced to do so? Sadists, torturers and terrorists are all people who find some way of justifying the fact that they hurt others. What is it that makes for that mentality? How does someone come to such a place; were they the sort of children that reveled in tormenting bugs? How does someone stay in such a mode of behavior when most people would refuse to undertake it in the first place? Will we ever understand, let alone prevent, suicide bombers?

Conversely, someone who purposely seeks out pain in one form or another is also an intriguing study. In the novel *Crash* by J. G. Ballard and subsequent film (by David Cronenberg, not the Paul Haggis film about racial tensions), people fetishize being injured in car wrecks; it's actually sexual for them. In *Dispatches*, the brilliant Vietnam war memoir by David Herr (a resource for the film *Apocalypse Now*), a photographer who has been serially injured by getting too close to the front lines stands naked before a mirror laughing uproariously at his scars, fractures and wounds.

How humans cope with what we experience, what we make from the remains of disaster, the choices we engage in that enliven or dull us, are all aspects of pain. It's easy to overlook the less obvious sides of pain, such as ticklishness.

Ticklishness is an aspect of personality and bodily response worth playing with on behalf of a character. On the surface it's simple: somebody is either not terribly ticklish or they can be reduced to ashes in a split-second even by the threat of being tickled. But to probe deeper into your character's reactions in this situation is to look at their entire physical being from the perspective of skin-as-self and pain-as-self.

Why do some people instantly break out into goose bumps if it's too cold for them, or their lips start chattering? Further, how is it that if someone else says it's cold, the listener suddenly feels chilled as well? Why are others immediately thrown into turmoil by being touched by a stranger or even by being tickled by someone they know well? I've witnessed someone actually become violent when they were tickled. Is our skin, our flesh, also our personality? Is an extreme reaction to tickling a function of emotional recall in someone with an abusive background or simply a powerful rejection by their skin and mind? Is the person whose lips are turning blue on a winter's day really experiencing that great a degree of cold or is it really a mental process? What if they don't feel the cold at all? Can we think ourselves warm? Or create a sense of coolness on a very hot day? How much control might your character have over their physical state of being? How do the people who can walk on hot coals do so? What about people who seem not to feel even physical pleasure?

In the film *Network*, Faye Dunaway's character, Diana Christensen, is head of programming for the fictional network UBS. She goes away for a lover's tryst with the film's protagonist, Max Schumacher, but even while they are making love—or rather while he is making love to her—she is ceaselessly talking about her work, seemingly without the slightest physical awareness of Schumacher's caresses. It's a brilliant bit of writing. The character is a compelling power broker and a beautiful woman, yet she seems utterly indifferent to physical pleasure. What impact would this have on your character? To carry it even further, what if your character is a woman who has undergone the utterly barbaric practice of female "circumcision"?

In this age of Viagra, many men can overcome genital difficulties but not all. There are so many variations on what can impact a man's ability to function, including diseases such as diabetes, or alcoholism and drug abuse. In addition, some medicines, including some antidepressants, can cause problems. Stress, anxiety and past sexual trauma can also be factors. While not necessarily a matter of physical pain per se, there's a direct correlation between dysfunction and the achievement of sexual fulfillment.

In the cultural realm of experiencing or tolerating pain, it's well known that certain indigenous people have rituals in which coming-of-age is established by enduring what amounts to a form of torture. Having one's body pierced, handling extremely hot things, body and face scarring, and many other practices abound throughout the world. Many of these are associated with religious observances that encourage martyrdom and sacred delirium. I remember seeing a documentary about a place where men are willing to reenact the crucifixion of Jesus by actually having their hands and feet pierced by spikes. It's hard to imagine how one might be willing to go this far, but it happens. In a similar vein, people will crawl up the steps of a cathedral or self-flagellate for penance, undertake a very arduous trek for the Muslim Hajj, or do prostrations over long stretches leading to temples to purify their karma.

We see aspects of this kind of behavior in various stories. In Steven Sondheim and Hugh Wheeler's *Sweeney Todd: The Demon Barber of Fleet Street*, Judge Turpin self-flagellates to purge impure thoughts; in the film *The Da Vinci Code*, the monk Silas punishes himself with a metal cilice, a device that bites into his leg painfully. There are milder examples, of course. In a brief scene in *American Beauty*, Annette Bening's character slaps herself for becoming emotional when she can't close a real estate deal. It's a small moment but highly effective and very telling about her character.

Pain is inevitable. How your character reacts to it, relates to it, or copes with it are aspects of personality well worth doing a full range of explorations. Even examining a person who attempts to avoid pain in every possible way can provide great results for your work. If we keep the definition of pain very broad, the mania for plastic surgery and the like is about fending off personal or social judgment about their appearance or the effects of aging. Perhaps in modern times, Joseph Merrick would have been able to transform into an Adonis with enough surgeries. Most of us watched the late Michael Jackson transmute himself over the decades, wondering at whether there might be an eventual stopping point for the work he persisted in having done. Would your character be someone who could also be so obsessed or even attempt to match Jackson's reworked face? What are the limits of what someone will endure in this kind of circumstance? If you've seen Terry Gilliam's film *Brazil*, you know he surmised that there would be a point of no return for perpetual rounds of plastic surgery.

Emotional pain is not exactly an element of touch but then again we can always look at everything from a variety of perspectives. Someone who suffers from an absolute fear of being judged might shut themselves away from society, which ultimately means doing without human contact. In Japan, there is a phenomenon known as *hikikomori*, which is when an adolescent or adult completely withdraws from society and lives in absolute isolation. There are many reasons for this, but from the variety of sources I looked at, the core is that the person has experienced some form of social trauma and withdrawn from the world. It's hard to imagine that contact with others is that dreadful and harder to comprehend denying oneself any physical interaction with others. To me, that seems like pain created to fend off pain and it leads me to wonder whether the actions of adolescents is universal, except in the way in which they respond to what they suffer. In America it seems that violence is the choice at times, though social isolation can happen on many levels. It's certainly true that many people set their outer, social personas in high school for survival and never fully leave the character they felt the need to play. Delving into the world of a character at that time of life, whether as current or investigation of the past, could bring a wealth of insights to your work.

As we see here, the range of potential explorations and discoveries related to pain is exceptional. And it may simply be true that the sense of touch is that encompassing as well. When we taste or use our other senses, touch is often involved on a very active basis without our recognizing it because our body is always scanning itself to see if everything is okay. Touch is all around us.

Touch Loss/Super Touch Etude

It is actually possible to lose your sense of touch. There's a condition known as peripheral neuropathy where the nerves that transmit the sense of touch to the brain are injured or destroyed. According to the website Wellescent.com, "Peripheral nerve injury can cause both signals to be lost and invalid signals to be sent. This is because the nerve damage often involves the protective layer on the surface of nerve cells rather than simply a break between nerve cells."[30] The effects can be a loss of sensation, or a feeling of numbness or tingling, normally in the hands or the feet. This condition can also be caused by the impact of certain diseases on the body, such as diabetes, hepatitis C and HIV/AIDS, as well as the side effects

---

30. Wellescent.com. "Peripheral Neuropathy Is More Than the Loss of Touch." Accessed 5 October 2014. http://wellescent.com/health_blog/peripheral-neuropathy-is-more-than-the-loss-of-touch.

of chemotherapy. According to the article, millions of people are afflicted with this condition from these sundry causes.

What impact would this have on a given character? It's difficult to imagine what it might be like not to be able to feel the world we encounter or to be unable to trust oneself to handle objects or even our children for fear of dropping them.

Six Degrees . . .

Your explorations do not have to be utterly faithful to the medical condition, of course. It might be interesting to create a circumstance in which someone's ability to feel touch is linked to their psychology or the situation in which they find themselves. This opens up comic or even surrealist possibilities. It's helpful to remember that with any etude you can pursue it as a real-life element or push it out to the most ridiculous places possible. Sometimes the discovery you make is by finding out what something is not, rather than what might be on too simplistic a level.

To play with this for a character, suppose that their sense of touch only goes away intermittently or for just an odd part of the body. We've all experienced numbness in our feet, legs or even backside from sitting too long. What if your character has a bad case of CKN—chronic knee numbness—or LESCPS—left ear sudden crazy prickly sensation? The possibilities are endless. In the film *Splash*, the character Dr. Walter Kornbluth (Eugene Levy) is determined to find a mermaid. In his pursuit he gets injured in various ways, including accidentally jabbing himself in the leg with a needle full of novocaine, and ends up having to drag the numbed leg along.

The other side of the coin might liberate you. Examine what happens when someone experiences a sense of super touch. In the Woody Allen film *Sleeper*, the future world is presented as dependent on machines to a great extent, such as a cabinet called the "orgasmatron," which provides a high-speed sexual experience, and an orb which makes the person extremely stoned. Once Allen's character, Miles Monroe, defrosted from cryogenic preservation after 200 years, experiences these devices he doesn't want to stop, even opting to fight off someone who is trying to get him to pass the orb.

It's possible that we've all experienced highly delightful touch, though perhaps not on the scale of the orb. Certainly the feel of a bit of fabric or an animal's fur or the splash of a wave on a hot summer day could all be moments in which we experience a sort of super touch. If we investigate the experiences of a character in this realm and then extend the sensations out to their extreme, many possibilities of expanding personality start to emerge.

However you choose to investigate the possibilities of touch, you will discover elements of your character that might never have surfaced otherwise. The range from the first kinds of touch one experiences at birth and after, to the way in which physical contact invites so many choices and opportunities in our lives is a wide-open world to tap into. You can approach it at the most fundamental level of how one feels in their clothes or the body itself on a given day. You can take it all the way out to the highest levels of stimulation in all manner of contexts and come back bearing gold.

As we will see in Chapter 6, our imaginations and ability to recall things in a sensory way can open doors for us. By working in this fashion we can deepen and broaden our characters, and in turn enrich our scripts.

Fade Out

How do others experience touch? How do your family members react to various kinds of contact? Are any of them people who cannot stand to be tickled or hugged?

For this fade out, you simply need to spend some quiet time thinking about the people you've known in your life and what their behavior has told you about their sense of contact. Certainly you can talk with others about this and reap much insight. The simplest way is to utilize your awareness of others and bring forward your memory of them.

For example, I once observed a person who was terribly anxious all the time. They would touch their face, hair and shoulder in sequence, over and over, looking almost like a baseball coach giving signals. It was hard to talk to this person because doing so only accelerated the self-touch. Another person I had a chance to watch was extremely passive, to the point of hardly moving as they worked at their desk. This person's handshake was disturbing because they didn't even attempt to grip my hand; it was like shaking hands with a mannequin.

Some people like to touch us. We like contact from one person but not from another. Try to recall the ways in which your family members may have touched you over the years, or friends, lovers, etc. What was in the nature of certain people's contact that was pleasurable or maybe not so much? What is it that Jimmy Stewart feels when he shakes Mr. Potter's hand in *It's a Wonderful Life*? Is it just cold and clammy, or is there some other quality that we would ascribe to it?

What did you experience after being injured in some way? I once lost control of my bicycle on a country road, flipped over and cracked a rib. I had to perform in a play that night and getting a full enough breath to project my voice was really painful. Are you a slow healer? Do you have a perpetual medical issue with some part of your body? Do you know someone who does? How do you or they cope?

To give really dedicated focus to all the pleasures, miseries and mysteries of touch is giving yourself the opportunity to know your body and those of others in the real world. Applying the insights that follow will bring your character's dimensionality into fuller perspective.

In the larger sense, something that touch does on a constant basis is to define the difference between others and ourselves, as well as where we share likenesses. Once you focus on treating your characters as real beings with all of the senses available to them to one degree or another you will have truly enlivened people in your scripts.

CHAPTER FIVE

Vision
The Sky Begins at Our Feet

"Vision is the art of seeing the invisible."
—Jonathan Swift, author

"Vision without action is a daydream. Action without vision is a nightmare."
—Japanese proverb

"The job of the artist is always to deepen the mystery."
—Francis Bacon, painter

"The question is not what you look at, but what you see."
— Henry David Thoreau, author

How do we see, what do we choose to see or avoid, and what do we know about our visual habits and preferences? How can we apply our understanding of vision and visualization to our writing? Alexandra Horowitz, in her book *On Looking*, tells us: "We see, but we do not see; we use our eyes but our gaze is glancing, frivolously considering its object. We see the signs, but not their meanings. We are not blinded, but we have blinders."[31]

Our realms, theatre and film, share many commonalities having to do with sight, with how the eye is directed and even how the eye is fooled.

---

31. Horowitz, *On Looking*, 40.

Chapter Five

Twenty-four frames per second. Two hundred watts fading up in five seconds to 50 percent. Light and the ability of the eye to perceive it in film (24 fps creates the illusion of motion from a sequence of still images) and on stage. If you don't know much about stage lighting, it's far more complex than you might imagine and well worth learning about. These aspects of the movie and theatre worlds are the most naturally linked to our visual sense because we go to *watch* a play or a movie (even if we do so in an auditorium; by definition a place for hearing). They are also the most commonly understood elements for screenwriters and playwrights, even though we may not talk about them in our scripts as such, but convey them when we indicate the mood, intensity, and emotion that our stories evoke. Light can convey atmosphere because of the way in which our eyes perceive light-as-meaning. What we experience in the day-to-day of our existence is based on the kind of light through which we move. When the day is over and we go from office fluorescence to softer light at home, and then out to a candlelit dinner, we are moving through visual states that create an awareness of how we are to behave or feel.

In theatres, we sit in the dark and witness a world conveyed to us through various kinds of light. If we could sit behind the movie screen and look through it, we'd see the eyes of the audience all moving in tandem as the camera and editing dictate, as the shapes of light and shadow demand. The same is true in theatre, though the audience has much greater liberty to experience the stage in an individual way, much as someone looks at a painting. We may choose to watch the actor speaking or the actor(s) listening or take in an element of the set or costumes, and so on. What we see on stage is more subjective by and large, though careful design and staging will always help to maintain focus on what's key to the telling of the story. Regardless, if light is not being reflected back to our eyes off the bodies, costumes, set pieces, etc., there's nothing to experience.

The way in which we encounter the world is dictated by what our eyes perceive. Our visual sense is our greatest defensive weapon among the senses, seconded by our ears. It is also a tremendous source of our life's pleasures. Our ability to see beauty is a major element of existence, even if we can't always define what is beautiful about what we're looking at in a given moment.

Vision

When I lived in New York, I had an unobstructed view from a sixth-floor apartment. I could see a high-rise three blocks away and sometimes I liked to sit in the dark and watch the TV lights in all those apartments flicker in counterpoint patterns. Now and then, if there was a major event, most of the TV lights would be blinking in synch. There was great beauty in those flashing screens for me; I had a deep sense of other lives going on, all with stories I loved to imagine. In spring and summer evenings, I liked to sit out on my fire escape and look west toward New Jersey, and watch the sun flame and color the long stretch of 13th Street. There's nothing more beautiful than a lingering sunset, except the ocean, or a log fire, or the faces of children, or—well, you get the picture.

In this age of selfies and incessant visual stimulation from our devices, how we perceive and use our sense of vision is in perpetual evolution. My students, most of whom are dedicated gamers, appear to be able to see things on a screen at a rate I cannot. I can't keep up and it makes me wonder if the way in which we see, the speed of perception, has changed over the millennia. I doubt if eyes have per se, but rather our brains' reception of what our eyes can take in at a given point must have changed as the technological world around us has.

I often talk to my students about the way in which the first people must have created theatre based on tales of survival around a fire in front of the cave, as the terror of darkness sat wrapped around them. Tiger-Slayer acts out how he killed the beast; everyone takes heart in the flickering light. Still, those eyes could see very little in the immense darkness and tigers could come at night, so no matter how reassured, imaginations were still racing. The next day, though, when Tiger-Slayer led a hunting party to bring home food, the pace at which things happened in the moment of confronting their prey was vastly heightened; a very different sense of looking.

Vision is so critical to our script-based arts that we hold a single adage as the very highest: "Show, don't tell." I encourage my screenwriting students to write as if the audience is comprised of those who cannot hear. In going through scripts, I demonstrate how a given moment full of chatter could be conveyed by a series of well-juxtaposed images. The adage applies slightly less to theatre because it's mostly a language-driven medium but there's no question that an unspoken moment can convey much more emotion and meaning than words, if the image is realized in such a way that the audience feels it.

Which immediately leads to the difficulty of thinking and writing in largely visual terms, regardless of medium.

The trap of "show, don't tell" lies in how people often mistake the word "show" for the verb "to demonstrate." I might ask a student why a description in the script says that a character is looking at their watch. "I want to show that they're worried about the time," the student responds. When I explain that all they're doing is demonstrating that the character will look at their watch at a given moment, I often get perplexed looks. There's a helpful conversation about this sort of thing in David Mamet's *On Directing Film*, which can certainly have applications for the stage.

I think we need to find a better word to replace "show." Perhaps "share, don't tell"? Or, more likely: "Visually engage the emotions and sensibility of the audience in an instant of human behavior that reveals something about what's going on inside the character, based on what we have a sense of about them, and need to know in order to connect with the emotional life, stakes and objectives for the character." Yes, that's probably better. Doesn't fit on a tee shirt so well, but hey.

The point is that the audience comes to observe, but even more so to experience, to gather images, words and actions in order to grasp the story as it accrues and feel the story in fundamentally human terms. There are very few moments when an audience isn't watching what's happening on the stage or screen. As we watch, the 24 fps or the ways in which things are framed and staged create a persistence of vision that is story. The deeper level of this persistence is that what we are observing is the breathing life of other human beings.

In the theatre, this creates an actual level of risk: the actors could come off the stage and attack us, or drag us into the play. This was a working concept for some of 1960s experimental work. Devotees of Brecht and Artaud, among others, we wanted to shatter the illusory "fourth wall" and eliminate the artificial boundary between audience and performers. Our ambition was to connect, teach and provoke meaningful interaction. The original production of *Hair* was infamous for people being invited onstage to disrobe in a Bacchanalian moment.

Vision

Woody Allen took this up on behalf of film in *The Purple Rose of Cairo*, but of course we know that movie characters can't come out of the screen to meet us, though we might desire it on some level. What happens instead is that close-ups give the okay to stare at someone's face, 3-D images seem to know where we are in the dark, and the fourth wall lives on to protect us. Naturally, we don't think about this very much; we sit in our seats feeling quite safe, comfy voyeurs.

In all regards, we are phenomenal observers. Many of us can tell in an instant if our loved one is upset or happy. We can identify a friend two blocks away, walking away from us, just by their movement and silhouette. We have a wide perspective on the space around us and can easily notice something moving around on the periphery of our vision. We can watch TV and be aware of other visual elements in our space.

To apply our observational powers to our writing requires that we give serious thought to how we see. A friend is blind in one eye. I spent some time walking around with one eye covered, to see what it was like. It was terrifying, especially going down stairs. It made me realize that a great part of my vision is about what I choose to see based on whatever limitations my eyes have. This can include a great many things, especially all forms of art.

Photographers are people I have great admiration for, so I have studied work by personal heroes such as Diane Arbus and Ralph Eugene Meatyard, who each had a phenomenal eye for weirdness, or Ansel Adams for his ability to capture landscapes in black and white like no one else ever has. David Douglas Duncan, after photographing World War II and the Korean War, finally had had enough glorifications of war and created works called *I Protest* and *War Without Heroes*, heartbreaking photographic protests against the Vietnam conflict.

I seek out all kinds of art. Modern dance, with its astonishing display of human plasticity, costuming and innovative lighting tells me as much about beauty and how other humans see the world as do paintings by Edgar Degas and Jean-Michel Basquiat, sculptures by Christo and Jeanne-Claude and Auguste Rodin, and so on.

How do we see, what do we choose to look at? What do we avoid or refuse to see? As John Henshaw observes, vision is " . . .

the only sense we can turn off."[32] When it isn't turned off, how are we using it? More importantly, how are your characters using their vision? We see billions of images during our lifetimes; why do we remember some and not others? There's a general consensus on various Internet sites that we see about 24,000 commercial ads in our lives. If we stop for a few seconds and try to recall them, why do some come instantly and others not at all? If we do the same with memories—visualize birthday parties you've attended in your life so far, recall the faces of as many friends as you can—we realize that there are bottomless files in our brains for these things.

When we play with this on behalf of our characters, we can open up paths into their worlds we had no notion existed. Ultimately, one of the fascinating things about what we artists do is start from a single spark of some kind—an image, a feeling, etc.—and build from there. So did the idea for the film *Amélie*, written by Jean-Pierre Jeunet and Guillaume Laurant, start from the image of the mysterious photo booth pictures or a garden gnome or some other source? It doesn't matter but it is fun to speculate about, especially since *Amélie* is a film that is far more based on what and how the characters see than many others.

Taken all in all, our visual sense may trump all the others we possess as scriptwriters. In the following etudes, I'm offering a smattering of possibilities. I urge you to go in as many directions with these as you can think of, combine them with other sense etudes and truly open the magnificent panoply of possibilities.

Key Etude: 20/20 Or ?

How are your eyes? Do you see well or need glasses? Have you had, or might you have, laser surgery or lens replacement? Can you see things at a distance but anything within two feet is a wad of cotton candy? Or vice versa? Do you have night blindness or severe sensitivity to the sun or bright light?

Whatever your response, it may be that these same questions about your character(s) will produce exciting possibilities for developing plot elements. It may also result in giving your character a

---

32. Henshaw, *A Tour of the Senses*, 79.

bit of a unique quality or quirk that provides a touch of texture to their personality.

The issue of sight is a treasure trove of exploratory possibilities. If a character needs glasses and is resistant, or if a character has a peculiarity of vision that shapes the world in a different way than anyone else, or if a character has perfect eyesight that is suddenly threatened by a physical disability of some kind, you have a personality with a clear and immediate problem.

Henshaw observes that "Glasses have existed since at least 1300."[33] With a history that deep, we could certainly investigate any number of possibilities. In Conor McPherson's play *The Seafarer*, the entire plot turns on what happens when a missing pair of glasses is found. In *Some Like it Hot*, Tony Curtis' character steals glasses from Joe E. Brown's character to pretend to be a nebbishy millionaire. And who would Harry Potter be without his glasses? Conversely, in a quote attributed to Dorothy Parker, it was long accepted that "Men seldom make passes at girls who wear glasses." Not true, of course, but I do notice the occasional young woman squinting to see the board in my classroom and wonder if she's leery of wearing glasses in public or even has them.

What underlies the refusal to get glasses? Is it vanity, a fear of doctors, a fear of having one's eyes touched in any way? Perhaps it's a genuine reluctance to seeing the world in reality, as if the character wants to live in a literal state of impressionistic dots and blurs. What might drive any of those choices? Family history, a childhood trauma, or worship of a particular school of painting are just a few of the possibilities. However it might play out, you can possibly find something anomalous about your character that might open up insights that you never had before.

Six Degrees . . .

There are a number of variations you can explore based on problems with vision other than myopia or the like. Vincent Van Gogh's eyesight is an example of extreme. It is speculated that he suffered from lead poisoning because of the paints he used—and lead

---

33. Ibid., 105.

poisoning can make someone see auras around lights—and that he may have been treated with a drug called digitalis, which can create yellow spots and a yellow haze in the vision. Some accounts dispute both assertions but the point is that Van Gogh saw the world in ways that others didn't.

If you research the kinds of things that can have an impact on vision, disorders such as diabetes, macular degeneration, glaucoma and cataracts, for some examples, you will find a range of problems for a character that may affect or inhibit their behavior. Imagine a cop who suffers from large floaters—moving spots that appear in one's vision field—trying to deal with chasing people on the street. I have floaters and in the summer I get a little bothered because there always seems to be a bug whizzing by, when it's just the tiny spots sliding around in my vision. The same issue might hold true for the cop who has difficulty with night vision, a problem for most people as they age.

There are other, more grim causes of eye problems such as detached retina, optic neuritis or a brain tumor. A character who is going blind due to a serious illness suffers greatly; perhaps a surgeon or a cinematographer suffers even more. There are stories of nobility in those circumstances, as well as plots that deal with the much darker aspect of human nature. What if a surgeon hopes to steal healthy eyes to replace their own? It can't be done with the entire eye in reality, but why not explore the fantastical possibilities? One of my dear friends, Ira Mazer, a phenomenal photographer, designated his cornea to be donated when he died. I couldn't help but speculate if the person who received his cornea could see the way Ira had. Not possible, of course, just a wish for my friend to live on in some fashion, so I wrote a play about it.

Color-Blindness Etude

According to Diane Ackerman, "Most people can identify between 150 and 200 colors. But we do not all see exactly the same colors, especially if we're partly or completely color-blind, as many people are—men in particular."[34]

---

34. Ackerman, *A Natural History of the Senses*, 252.

Now, it would be easy to merely work with a character who can't distinguish one color from another. It's good stuff. Look at the character of Dwayne in *Little Miss Sunshine*, who discovers his color-blindness accidentally, followed by the immediate realization that something for which he has sacrificed greatly—to fly planes for the Air Force—has suddenly and irremediably come to a crashing halt. It's a sobering moment in the film.

Color-blindness can easily be the stuff of comedy as well. The guy who can't tell which girl is wearing the red dress he is supposed to look for; a woman who buys her boyfriend orange pants, thinking they're green, and off he goes to a St. Patrick's Day parade.

But color-blindness can also be looked at more broadly as a genuine challenge to someone's life that isn't part of a sweet family movie or romantic comedy. Peter Milton, a painter and teacher, discovered his color-blindness at the age of thirty-two. It forced him to go into black-and-white drawing and printmaking, which was far from the worst thing that could have resulted, as his art work will readily show (this information comes from a story on NPR: http://www.npr.org/2014/11/16/364092778/for-one-artist-colorblindness-opened-up-a-world-of-black-and-white; the article includes some of Milton's exquisite prints).

Color-blindness could also be a factor in the world of a chef or a clothing designer, but also just in the day-to-day realities of life. The parent who cannot see certain colors might greatly disappoint a proud child by not being able to appreciate the painting brought home from school.

You may be color-blind and not realize it, in fact. I have difficulty telling gray from green unless the shade of each is really bright. For years I drove a van that I saw as gray but everyone told me was green; I thought it was a joke in my family for a long time until people I wasn't related to started telling me the same thing.

Six Degrees . . .

A different kind of "eye" problem is emotional or psychological blindness. This is related to color-blindness in a figurative way: seeing in black-and-white terms with regard to other beings. The inability to feel empathy or to see the reality in which one is living is rooted in stories and myths from far back in history. The character Tiresias in *Oedipus Rex* is physically blind but clairvoyant. He can see what Oedipus cannot because the king suffers from extreme pride—hubris—that makes him blind to the truth and ultimately leads to Oedipus' self-blinding.

Psychological blindness is one of the most potent obstacles for a character. The character who cannot accept the circumstances in which they exist is classic. Dr. Eldon Tyrell, in *Blade Runner*, cannot see the harm he has done by giving bioengineered beings (called replicants) human feelings and desires; he is shown in the film wearing symbolically oversize, thick-lensed glasses. In the film *Nightcrawler*, Jake Gyllenhaal's character is afflicted with blind ambition, another kind of psychological blockage that runs through many stories for stage or screen. This condition can be examined in any number of ways.

Whatever it may be that prevents a character from seeing with clarity, in any regard, can be wonderful material for your explorations. It will help to keep in mind that these things can easily be interrelated: a person suffering from the psychological blindness of a doggedly competitive overachiever may be the very type that cannot countenance having their eyes checked.

You can broaden a character of this type by moving them into other circumstances. What's that blind overachiever like in the sandbox in preschool or in the retirement home? When did their psychological blindness begin? What caused it? Most critically: when are they offered, as is Oedipus, the opportunity to see and what happens if they accept or refuse?

Color Etude

The purpose of this etude is to look at the way in which characters are understood on the basis of color, the way in which the characters find color attractive, or not, and the way in which the color around the characters has an impact. Some of the work in this etude is to have a good look at your own sense of color; the rest has to do with how you deal with color on behalf of your characters, plots and even thematic elements.

In the *Three Colors Trilogy*, directed by Krzysztof Kieślowski, the colors referenced in the title are blue, white and red, which are those of the French flag in order from left to right, representing the ideals of the French Revolution: liberty, equality and fraternity.

In the film *Blue Velvet*, by David Lynch, the color blue suggests a state of mind—a young man's tormented blues caused by unrealized desires—and possibly the dark neo-noir mood of the movie itself.

In *Schindler's List*, an absolutely heartbreaking image is that of the tiny girl in the red coat, in stark juxtaposition to a world that is largely colorless. It is a powerful visual that gains meaning further into the film on levels that other moments strive to match.

In the theatre, the typical light plot will have warm gels (leaning toward orange) on one side and cool blue gels on the other which, when mixed, give a feeling of natural light. Sets are painted in colors that often have less to do with recreating reality than providing a color metaphor for the world. The musical *Sunday in the Park with George* is a celebration of the work of Georges Seurat, the neo-impressionist painter. The usual backdrop of the production is a reproduction of Seurat's famous painting "A Sunday Afternoon on the Island of La Grande Jatte," which provides a wealth of color reference throughout the play.

Exploring color on behalf of our characters, plots and thematic qualities can be highly provocative and productive work.

As usual, begin with yourself. What colors do you like in your life? Are you fond of subtle, muted colors in your home? Do you like to dress in vivid hues when you go out at night but during the day you choose to be more corporate (and seriously, what in the world is "business casual")? Are you a devotee of the all-black NYC East Village look? Do you like to change your hair color frequently? When you do, is it to a natural shade that's lighter or darker, or do you go for absolute peacock?

Are you willing to admit that you have no color taste at all? Is that you in the blue jeans with brown socks, black lace-up shoes and an age-yellowed white shirt? Come on, 'fess up.

"What's in your closet?" is the question fashion shows like to ponder. What do you wear to sleep in or to change into that's just for hanging around the house? Are you, as one friend said of another, afraid of color? What's your idea of sexy in clothing? If you think about yourself at a point when you were pretty clueless or indifferent about color, you can apply that to your character. You can summon that one detail that might make you squirm in embarrassed recollection or that will give you a warm sense of satisfaction, and let that be the key thing you indicate in the script.

I hope you're laughing at this point. Personal taste is a funny thing, after all. You may be the most "fashion-forward" person in the world or you might have long ago succumbed to comfort, without the slightest interest in whether what you're wearing matches or is without holes. You may be the one who goes through whatever's piled on the floor in your bedroom, sniffing each piece to see what's the least smelly, or you may be the person who cannot leave home without spending many minutes getting everything just right.

Has your taste or your perspective on colors in your clothing altered as you've gotten older? In Jenny Joseph's poem "Warning," the narrator looks forward to wearing purple and red in her old age as a statement of vigorous defiance against convention and ageist preconceptions.[35] From the inspiration of this poem arose the Red Hat Society, an organization intended to help create bonding and communication among women. Seeing a group—a flock, perhaps—of women in these hats, complimented with all manner of purples and other opulent shades, is a remarkable sight.

It's always helpful to get to know designers in theatre and film when you can. Their take on the interactions between lights, costumes and setting is going to be very informative. In particular, they will tell you that color is related to the era in which people existed. In the 1960s, many of us enjoyed dressing in nonconformist clothing. In the current day, young people like the hippie look but many don't really understand the powerful liberation the clothing represented, so it's mimicry. This is only natural, of course, but we all owe it to our characters to have a fuller understanding of what clothing and color mean to them in their time and milieu. It's well worth your time to seek out a variety of resources on design, since the visual aspect is not limited to color but such aspects as line, structure, texture and so on.

As you become more aware of your own taste, the extension is into greater familiarity with the taste of your character. We must keep in mind always that we write for two receptors: the audience and our collaborators. You don't help things by describing a

---

35. Joseph, Jenny. "Warning." Accessed 12 October 2014. http://www.barbados.org/poetry/wheniam.htm.

character from head to toe in your script, though there's no prohibition for doing so other than common sense. If you're truly respectful of your eventual designers you learn to focus on the salient detail that will be a solid clue to those who will actually realize the look. Leave room for their art to engage with yours. For example, I once wrote only that a character had a "fatal attraction to red wedgies." The costume designer got that image as I'd hoped: just about everything the character wore was just a bit off, a bit gaudy, a shade too bright for her age and "type." It's a gamble, of course, to hope that the production of your work will land as you have visualized it, but all scriptwriters have to acknowledge that there is a letting-go point.

This advice applies also for describing a set or even the physical attributes of a character. Less is more, first of all, and respect for the other artists is critical. This might be a matter of saying she is wearing an elegant wine-colored dress, or he has the taste of an overgrown five-year-old, and leaving plenty of room for interpretation by the costumer. In a very real sense, the way in which you use descriptive language toward your eventual collaborators is a kind of poetry and something to be worked at diligently in your scripts.

Six Degrees . . .

When we expand this etude into the color of the world the characters occupy, we can enter the realm of artists whose entire oeuvre is visual. As you'll see in the Fade Out, I'm sending you to museums and libraries in search of art to use as inspiration. How is it that a given visual artist can find beauty in a pile of rocks most of us would simply pass by without noting much about it? When we look at the work of photographers whose images are in black and white, we experience another kind of eye, one that can translate the world of color into the range of tones between the two poles. This can apply to the Special Vision Etude later in the chapter as well.

The colors of the character's world are another design aspect. The more confident you are of those elements, the better. You'll be able to rein yourself in from overdoing it by learning to focus on what is the most crucial image. You may gain some benefit from looking at examples of Japanese flower arranging practice (*ikebana*) or other visually disciplined practices to gain some insight.

For instance, writing that a vase filled with several dozen red roses sits atop a dining table might just be enough to set a scene's emotional tone. Red roses connote the expression of love, generally speaking, though I don't think people speak the language of flowers as they once did; something else for you to investigate. Still, red roses are not inexpensive and the darkest red ones are very compelling to the eye. The color might be suggested as prelude to a romantic scene or you may think of it as ironic, in that the scene is not going to be happy and light and that the vase is going to end up smashed at some point, with roses everywhere. If you put the roses in a different room, everything changes: on a bureau in a cheap motel as opposed to in an extremely messy kitchen, or thrown into a bathtub, or unceremoniously tossed out a window. Still, by making the roses the focus of the space you have chosen something that communicates with the space and ultimately with the viewer. You could easily write a series of etudes based on stories related to red roses.

In addition—or alternatively—giving an indication of a room's color can be very helpful to you as you develop a given scene. It's your job to see the world of your characters as vividly as you can. I remember visiting the apartment of a very conservative businessman in New York. It was a production meeting and the businessman was investing in my play *Blood Relations*. After passing through the foyer to the apartment, we entered his living room. It was occupied by a beautiful black grand piano atop which was a vase with a white lily in it, looking serene. The walls were covered in very intense red and gold patterned wallpaper. It actually made me blink because the room was so set-like (track lighting helped this) and because the space seemed so utterly unlike the gray-suited man who owned it. If I wrote a script using this, I might skip the wallpaper in favor of the black-and-white combination of flower and piano; you might prefer the wallpaper.

The real question is what colors would suit your character's domicile? In the 1950s people liked the combination of pink and black, in clothing and cars, and even, as my mother did, in her kitchen's tiles and cookware. What's the right hue for their space and what other color might enter into it that might cause disruption? What kinds of things are on the walls where they live? Consider all possibilities: a loft space for an artist that is splattered with paint everywhere, with half-finished works sitting on easels and hanging on partitions versus a living room that is right out of some magazine illustration, where the wall decorations are chosen just for their color and not as truly valued artwork. Is the space filled to the brim with beautiful and meaningful objects? If you've never seen photos of Gertrude Stein's apartment, it's worth a quick Internet break. She was an avid collector of original paintings; they covered the walls and even the ceilings of her living space. Woody Allen's designers successfully duplicated this in his film *Midnight in Paris* when we meet Stein as one featured character; you get the sense that she loves being surrounded by friends, which includes the paintings. Could your character love a work of art in that personal way?

Another consideration is where the character is located on the planet. In Santa Fe the pinkish color of adobe homes is everywhere. As we discover from the paintings by Georgia O'Keefe, among others, Santa Fe and nearby environs have their own light and coloration. If you shift to Sweden, for example, you see a different quality of light—more blue, more stark.

In Diane Ackerman's book there is an intriguing discussion of color in particular cultures: "Primitive languages first develop words for black and white, then add red, then yellow and green; many lump blue and green together, and some don't bother distinguishing between other colors of the spectrum." She later adds: ". . . the Maori of New Zealand . . . have many words for red—all the reds that surge and pale as fruits and flowers develop, as blood flows and dries."[36] It may be that your character has an entire set of cultural realities underlying their sense of color and what color means in their world. Communicating that can be somewhat difficult but using it as an element in a script can be pure gold.

Ultimately, color is a useful element that has phenomenal resonance. Color creates emotional reactions in us; some subtle and others not so much. How you approach the use of color in your scripts will likely vary wildly based on the kind of story you're telling and the sort of people who populate it. You might find it very

---

36. Ackerman, *A Natural History of the Senses*, 253.

interesting to go back through scripts you've written or the work of others and look for color usage and cues.

In the opening screenplay pages of the first *Godfather* film, for example, there are a number of references to the color black: the script opens in black with a voiceover; the first person we see is Amerigo Bonasera, wearing a black suit; the Corleone archenemy Barzini arrives wearing a black homburg; Paulie brings Clemenza a glass of "icy black wine"; a little girl dances on the feet of Tessio, "her little black party shoes planted on his enormous brown shoes."[37] It seems as if touches of darkness and death are moving throughout the wedding celebration that has brought all the characters together.

Ultimately, even if your notion of color isn't used in the production, you have at the very least planted a thought. In the film, Bonasera's face fills the screen at first, seeming to float in a black void as the camera slowly pulls back, further extending the power of the color imagery in the script.

Why They're Looking Etude

It's our nature to let our eyes wander around any room we're in, depending on how interesting whatever's in front of us may be. In a state of boredom we may only be aware of the details of the room as a general mix. In a state of being focused, we can find ourselves taking things in with appreciation as they hold our attention or reflect our own values or aesthetics.

When someone has a vested interest in what's around them, the sense of vision is quite different. This is also true for someone who has been through some sort of trauma.

For example, a pickpocket's eyes are not likely to be better in terms of general vision, but have developed a kind of radar that alerts the thief to a likely score.

We can easily find variations on the multitude of ways in which eyes work and how they express the person's experiences.

A battle-weary, traumatized soldier returning from combat is often described as having a "thousand-yard stare." This dissociative

---

37. Coppola, Francis Ford, and Mario Puzzo. *The Godfather*. Screenplay. Accessed 17 October 2014. http://www.script-o-rama.com/snazzy/dircut.html.

gaze is the result of what used to be called shell shock, now known as post-traumatic stress disorder (PTSD). The look on the soldier's face is one of unadulterated despondence created by having witnessed too much to cope with.

A host or hostess may seem to have eyes that can see 360 degrees, as they try to keep the party moving along. Security people—ranging from private guards to the Secret Service—experience the same sense of omnidirectional awareness.

An assassin sees little but their target.

As Alexandra Horowitz describes, "There is a certain bias in everyone's perspective that has been named, by the French, *déformation professionnelle*: the tendency to look at every context from the point of view of one's profession. The psychiatrist sees symptoms of diagnosable conditions in everyone."[38]

Your character may not be a ninja or a shrink but will typically have some element of watchfulness or inward gazing that is the result of what they do and why they need to see in the particular way they do. We can sit loose to the term assassin: we apply it to an overzealous car salesman or perfume sniper.

Using this etude as a prompt might be a very helpful investigation into backstory. A character who might have the tendency toward continual eye shifting may simply be someone who worked for too long on a high-speed assembly line. Then again, they may have been a hit man or there's a congenital disorder creating the problem. How the person uses their eyes in the present may be a key to a background that could open up a variety of doors for your work.

Six Degrees . . .

My hope is that when you're writing an etude about a given character you'll find that you start to wonder how they became who they are, which is when this process can be very informative. In this instance, why they're looking is based on the confluence of current observation and memory. What they see before them may not look the same as it once did but there's a memory lodged in

---

38. Horowitz, *On Looking*, 3.

the sight; nonetheless, the looking can generate everything from a flashback to a liberation. Such actions are sometimes undertaken when someone is suffering from PTSD: revisiting the locale can allow the memory to reduce in power.

This does not have to focus on trauma, of course. I had a very disoriented feeling when I revisited Orlando, Florida, after not being there for more than twenty years. Not only were there an uncountable number of new stores and housing areas, but an entire stretch of apartment buildings, including one where I had lived, had been replaced by a highway. Some things were very recognizable, such as the magnificent downtown library, and brought back a wealth of pleasant reflections.

Still more striking was the area of land where McCoy Air Force Base—my permanent station, 1967–1970—had been. Once decommissioned, it had been completely razed and replaced by scores of industrial buildings. There was nothing left to grab hold of, except in memory, so even without visual reference I could still trace my steps from the barracks to the warehouse where I worked. I don't think about the base often but when I do it seems to be just where I left it after processing out in 1970—except in reality.

In those moments, I am seeing through the eyes of a pretty unwilling member of the military, as well as a young man happily experiencing life on his own for the first time. I could travel around the areas of Orlando and Winter Park recalling how things looked back then, not just visually but also based on how I felt at the time.

In other words, a jaded psychiatrist who looks at everyone as a potential diagnosis might do so in their current eyes or through much younger eyes—eyes that may not have yet become professionally trained or world-weary. They might be the eyes of someone realizing what they wanted to be for the first time, eyes that had not yet seen it all. We all have moments when we encounter our day in an ebullient state of mind, in a childhood state of happiness—something we can track for ourselves and on behalf of our characters. Conversely, we may experience a trigger that sends us back to a darker time that we—and our character—might not have realized was there, or had attempted to deny. If you have such a place, one that disturbs you, perhaps you could send a character as your emissary and find some relief. The range of what can be done with our writing is limitless.

Special Vision Etude

We watch in tense apprehension as Jame Gumb hunts Clarice Starling wearing night-vision goggles. Jonathan Demme, the director of *Silence of the Lambs*, used this sequence to great effect by shooting the terrifying scene from Gumb's point of view, inside the goggles.

In *The Hunt for Red October*, we see the world through the periscope. In the film *Syriana*, we view drone airstrikes via the computer screens that track them.

In Peter Shaffer's play *Black Comedy*, we watch people groping around the stage as if in utter darkness, the hook being that when the lights blow in the world of the play, the stage lights come on. Much of the humor is generated by what the audience can see that the characters cannot. In the play and film of *Wait Until Dark*, the blind heroine of the story manages to defeat the villain by plunging her apartment into darkness. She can navigate the space easily; he cannot.

In any of these instances, we are telling a story to our audience through some special limit or enhancement of vision.

We have to be careful not to simply cook up an excuse for special vision but have it be organic to the story we're telling and to the characters. In other words, even though Susy Hendrix defeats the bad guy in *Wait Until Dark* by "taking advantage" of her blindness, the story doesn't hold up if she just turns off the lights. She has to be resilient and tenacious, and the villain has to be resourceful and ruthless and he has to nearly succeed in killing her.

The way in which something provides a condition of unique, unorthodox or exceptional vision can be an intriguing exploration of metaphor, as well as character perspective. In *Silence of the Lambs*, Jame's night-vision goggles reveal a variety of things: 1) he is a professional stalker (gives me chills to consider that concept); 2) he regards what he does as a cat-and-mouse thing (after all, he could just leap on Starling first thing); and 3) in terms of metaphor, only someone as sociopathic as Jame knows what's truly in the heart of psychological darkness. The use of special vision as obstacle, upper hand or symbol brings layers to what we take for granted: the familiar trope of the periscope view in submarine films is a persistent reminder that the dual realities of submarines are simultaneously stealth and entrapment.

Chapter Five

One of the most claustrophobic films ever made is the very fine German movie *Das Boot*. The audience's experience of the film is of a world that is slowly collapsing inward, ready to implode at any moment, while the outside world only exists as a tiny, possibly unreliable image. The abundance of submarine films in the post–World War II era was perhaps a way of putting our vision directly into the world of war without the persistent gun and cannon fire of land battles. These films often work as much from the absence of sound, other than the sonar pinging, as they do from the absence of a full field of vision.

To play with this etude, give some thought to ways in which your character might see in a special way. An extreme introvert might only look at other people via reflective surfaces, for example. A narcissist might focus primarily on seeing their own reflection in the eyes and glasses of other people. A depraved scientist might invent glasses to see through people's clothes or ones that make people see them only in a positive way.

Six Degrees . . .

The start of this variation focuses on special vision from the perspective of a seer, prophet, psychic or clairvoyant. If we go back to Tiresias for a moment, we have a character who is a great archetype: the blind person who can truly "see" better than the sighted and know the truth. How does he know it's Oedipus that's the cause of the plagues on the town? We never get an answer to that because we grant him special vision: he's a seer; it's what they do.

Working with our characters on this basis can be great fun, especially if you aren't too literal. Yes, there are people who can read palms—I have a friend who can to an unnervingly accurate degree—but there are vastly more people who are just highly intuitive. They trust their gut. I once asked Moisés Kaufman where his ideas came from. He said, "I have a hunch." That was it.

Pseudointuitive characters overpopulate soap operas and bad TV scripting, unfortunately, and it's a struggle for teachers of writing to get their students to unlearn the tendency to use coincidence or sudden inorganic revelations. Out of the blue, Serenity knows that her husband Studly has been unfaithful. Well, yeah, that happens:

Vision 137

people get an intuitive feel for something and with some digging they find what they most fear or hope. Just don't make it too easy for your character to realize their hunch. You will learn even more about them depending on how hard it is to prove their intuition, how desperate they are to get at it.

That said, there's a long history of clairvoyants, palm readers and mystics of all stripes in both theatre and film. They are often depicted as charlatans, such as Whoopi Goldberg's brilliantly performed Oda Mae Brown in *Ghost*, or they are a plot twist, as in the character of Madame Arcati in Noel Coward's classic work *Blithe Spirit*, who makes an actual ghost manifest to great comic effect in the play.

A great many people believe in psychics and psychic phenomena. Perhaps your character only has a moment of clairvoyance but it shakes their assumptions about someone else to the core. Maybe your character pretends to be a palm reader for their kid's school carnival and discovers hitherto unknown secrets. Or they have read their own palm and unhappily know the future.

I haven't really referenced horror films often in this book. I don't like them because they actually scare me. *Psycho* was my last one for decades until *Carrie*, *The Shining* and *Silence of the Lambs*, which did me in permanently. The basis for a number of horror films is special vision, of course, so I encourage you to explore the possibilities therein. In this variation, special vision includes what a character sees, what the director lets us see—or not see—and what the aftermath of the horror is.

An angle on this is the unique vision related to someone who is mentally disturbed. One of the most underrated films in the psychological horror subgenre is Roman Polanski's *Repulsion* (1965). The film begins and ends with a close-up of an eye, possibly in homage to the shower scene in Hitchcock's *Psycho* (1960). In the course of *Repulsion* the main character, Carole Ledoux, played by Catherine Deneuve, is slowly going crazy. Images that Polanski uses to portray her descent include walls that suddenly crack, hands that reach out from the walls to grope her, and a repeated image of three buskers—street musicians—two of whom are bent over playing the spoons and the other more upright playing a banjo; they have no real purpose other than to suggest menace. Are they really there or merely her hallucination, like the cracking walls? In a wonderfully startling moment, a wardrobe mirror slowly swings open and we suddenly glimpse a man sitting on the bed. Just as quickly, the camera shows us he's not really there. Throughout the film another disturbing sequence is that of Carole's nightmares, in which someone is breaking into her room. Polanski removes the soundtrack entirely during these dreams—no hiss, no heavy-handed heartbeat—just an abrupt blankness of sound; it makes us feel as if our hearing has gone out, and we have joined Carole in the grip of the horrifying dream.

Repulsion is a great example of special vision. Polanski puts us in the visual reference of the character in such a way that we experience her deterioration. There are some point of view shots scattered through the film but mainly Polanski involves us by showing the way in which Carole experiences the world falling apart, the camera looking on impassively as real danger circles her increasingly disturbed state.

As you develop your characters and plots, pursuing the notion of special vision can be a very effective way of deepening your work or even shifting the angle of the story in such a way that we are drawn in more subjectively.

The main thing is to let the notion of special vision take you as far as you're willing to go. As with the other etudes in the world of seeing or the other senses, there are no limits except for those you allow or impose. If you revisit the key etude notion of asking others how they see, asking them about unique vision could open many avenues for you and possibly push aside any barriers you may have. Every family seems to have someone with either a unique visual difficulty or capability; you may strike gold.

Animal Eyes Etude

In other sense areas, I have suggested that approaching character through animal-like behavior could be of value. The same is emphatically true for vision.

If we examine the world of animals, we discover that the predators, including us, have eyes facing front, whereas those who are more typically prey have eyes on each side of their head. When a writer describes a character as "a young colt," we get the rambunctiousness of the person, that teenage willingness to throw the body heedlessly into space and circumstances. What we also get, by way of secondary image, is a sense of a highly vulnerable person, which everyone except the adolescent knows they are. In the natural world, evolution has provided prey animals with the tools needed to survive: exceptional speed, impossible-to-penetrate exteriors, and built-in stink bombs. In the human world, those who are prey may lack those special tools.

Where might your character fall within this range? In two films where characters face mirrors, we experience very different personalities. In *All That Jazz*, we see Bob Fosse's character, Joe Gideon, addressing himself in the glass each morning saying, "It's showtime," where in *The Hustler* the wrongly treated girlfriend, Sarah, played by Piper Laurie, looks at her reflection and feels only loathing and profound emptiness, writing "perverted" and "twisted" on the mirror in lipstick prior to taking her life. Gideon is a kind of predator; Sara a recognizable prey.

The way in which most of us learn about the world when we're very young is through tales of animals and anthropomorphized animal behavior, whether from Aesop or modern writers like Dr. Seuss or Richard Scarry. We learn that the rabbit is shy and skittish, the fox is a sharp-eyed hunter, the bear is a big sleepy mound of fur, and so on. As we get older we may develop a sense of other people via animal imagery. In fact, they may see themselves that way. I knew an actor who fancied himself quite the ladies' man and certainly never rested in his pursuit of women. One of his targets said, "So, you're a wolf in sheep's clothing." "Oh, no, my dear," he countered, "I'm a wolf in wolf's clothing."

John Henshaw, in his book *A Tour of the Senses*, describes something that snakes have, called a pit organ or pit hole: "The pit hole is a shallow depression located between the nostril and the eyes.... It allows the snakes to detect infrared radiation, an ability they put to good use hunting prey in the dark."[39] This description struck me as what certain human predators must have in their own fashion. Pimps and con artists, for example, know how to hunt for and take down a likely subject. It made me wonder if the vulnerability of the people who are victimized gives off a certain heat or aura that makes them easy to spot to these snake-humans.

Alternatively, perhaps hunters are more like Diane Ackerman's charming description of an owl, which she describes as "a pair of

---

39. Henshaw, *A Tour of the Senses*, 81.

binoculars with wings, whose eyes make up a third of its head size."[40] I had the experience of being able to touch an owl when I was living near a small village in England. There was a fete which included rescued owls for people to see close up. One of the handlers invited me to push my finger into the owl's feathers, showing me how far in from the outer feather surface the body of the owl was, by way of explaining why an owl is such a successful hunter: they move almost without any noise. So a character who has huge eyes (this can be metaphorical, of course) and moves with amazing silence might be precisely the kind of person who can sneak up, like Eve Harrington in *All About Eve*, on their prey with very little warning.

It can be great fun for you to explore your characters as animals. Keep in mind that this falls into how they see themselves as well as how they are seen. In recent parlance, a desirable woman may have been described as a "fox." Puttering around on the Internet about this, wondering about the origins, I came across a comment that made me laugh and here I paraphrase: women are called foxes because it's like a fox hunt when you hit the bars. Perhaps a woman might see herself this way? I have no clue, any more than I do about why calling women a female dog has become common coinage for both sides of the genders, something I'd like to see disappear soon.

Six Degrees . . .

We can also look at our characters as how they might function as herd animals. In *On Looking*, Alexandra Horowitz observes that there are three "rules" for beings that move in packs, whether we're talking about ants or birds or animals that migrate: "First, avoid bumping into others (while staying comfortably close). . . . The second rule: Follow whoever is in front of you. . . . The final rule: Keep up with those next to you."[41] If you live in a big city or you have to commute in any fashion during a rush hour anywhere, you recognize these rules for survival. In the film *Koyaanisqatsi: Life Out of Balance* we see the problem of group behavior all too clearly as life is shown speeding up more and more.

---

40. Ackerman, *A Natural History of the Senses*, 236.
41. Horowitz, *On Looking*, 146.

When writers take on aspects of crowd or mob mentality, we instantly recognize the danger that lurks there because the rules are suddenly out the window. In the Ibsen play *An Enemy of the People*, the protagonist, Dr. Stockman, has discovered that there are harmful microbes in the vaunted new health baths of the town. The leaders and citizens of the town are enraged to the point of violence that Stockman would reveal this truth and thereby ruin the anticipated economic boost the spa would generate. Ultimately, in spite of incredible opposition, Stockman elects to stand firm, knowing that he has made the moral choice.

We can see this pack behavior in so many other stories: *Twelve Angry Men*, *The Oxbow Incident* and the play and film by David Mamet *Glengarry Glen Ross*, among many others. In exploring a character who would either go along with the mob or stand against it, you have someone who reflects human nature in a profound way. If the character decides to break any or all of Horowitz's three rules, there's hell to pay and most of us don't have the courage to go there. When this is the situation, we are asking one of the great questions for all humanity: What choice should we make? In *The Year of Living Dangerously*, a key character asks this very question. Given that a leader has turned his back on the people, in effect on the pack, Billy Kwan asks: "What must we do?"

Another very simple and fun way to approach this etude is to go on to Facebook or any other social medium where people post videos of cute animal behavior or people acting in an animal-like fashion. This is largely dependent on your working definition of what animal behavior might entail. Make sure you suspend preconceptions. After all, the lovable bear of children's stories will actually maul you if you're in the wrong woods at the wrong time.

Standing in the Sky Etude

This etude series takes its title from another quote from Diane Ackerman: "Look at your feet. You are standing in the sky. When we think of the sky we tend to look up, but the sky actually begins at the earth."[42]

---

42. Ackerman, *A Natural History of the Senses*, 236.

I stopped and reread that segment about five times; how revelatory, how simple!

What we'll take a look at in this part of vision is the way in which we deal with our limitations, regardless of the cause. In effect, it is similar to the earlier sensory etudes that focus on a character having too much or too little of a given sense, such as the Much Nose or No Taste Etudes. This series of etude varieties focuses on aspects that, like the sky, are all around us and yet we rarely notice.

If you take the range of possibilities of, shall we say, super sight to super-poor sight, your character may have emotional qualities you hadn't suspected. The obvious is to refer to the Superman character with his X-ray eyes, but if we expand this, we can open out to the notion that your character has exceptional abilities to see the emotional state of another person.

In the Wim Wenders film *Wings of Desire*, we meet an angel named Damiel who wants to experience what he observes of human life in the city of Berlin. His passion to have direct knowledge of humanity leads him to set aside his immortality to taste food, see color, know love. Damiel is a supernatural being, so maybe we didn't get too far from Superman. Still, you may be someone who feels the emotions of other people very deeply or want to examine this as a possibility for a character.

There is a state of awareness in which someone is called an "empath," which, at its far pole is someone who can psychically tune in to the emotional experience of a person, place or animal, often involuntarily. On a more everyday level an empath is a person who cannot help but pick up on the emotions of others, which is the experience of a great many people. A simple way of looking at this is to see how you felt when someone you were near took a fall or got hurt in some dramatic way—if you felt ill or a sharp tingling in your body, you were being empathic in that moment. The same goes for feeling unbridled joy in the success of another. To play with this as an etude, imagine your character existing like this on a constant basis, so that whatever they saw could cause these wildly divergent sensations in their body. What would they do to exert some level of control over this kind of rebounding? Living alone might be one choice but how far from society must they go? Is your character likely to be the hermit in the hut on the mountainside? What if it works the other way and they have become an empathy junkie, constantly seeking out emotional experiences and feeding on them, vampire-like?

Then flip the condition and ask yourself what it would be like to feel nothing about other people; to be utterly indifferent to their happiness or suffering. It's hard to imagine such people, but of course this is all around us and has been since humans invented war. A quick visit to any of the films about the Holocaust can readily serve as a reminder: *Night and Fog*, *Shoah* and so on. In the classic 1979 comedy-drama *Being There*, Chance, the main character, is a virtual cypher: having no real understanding of the world, he is a perfect blank slate for others to inscribe with their "reading" of him. The poster for the film shows Chance, played by the inimitable Peter Sellers, walking in the sky, as if he's unaware of even the laws of gravity. In modern western theatre, plays such as Neil LaBute's *Fat Pig* and David Mamet's *Edmond* have examined the degree to which humans can lose empathy for others.

The middle ground of this is to examine the way in which your character looks at things based on context. Do they see the homeless people around them? Do they experience unfettered joy for another or jealousy? In *Rachel Getting Married*, the characters of sisters Kim and Rachel are wonderful studies of how people can go in and out of empathy as a given circumstance evolves. We are all subject to an overwhelming minefield of input on a daily basis just listening to the news; it's amazing that any of us are relatively sane.

Six Degrees . . .

A variant on empathy can be looked at from a medical condition perspective. Someone with Parkinson's dementia, for example, tends to lose their facial expressiveness over time. A different disorder is known as face blindness: how well someone is able to know another's face on sight. This ranges from "super-recognizers" to people who are face blind. "Super-recognizers" is a term that John Henshaw uses in his book *A Tour of the Senses* to describe someone with the ability to remember a face from a previous time, regardless of the relationship. He describes his stepdaughter: "She can pass someone in a crowd at the airport and remember him as the waiter who served her a restaurant meal a few years back." He continues:

"At the lower end of the curve are the severely face blind, who are sometimes unable to recognize the faces of family members or even of themselves."[43]

As we get older we tend to have more difficulty remembering names and faces, so most of us are somewhere on the spectrum that Henshaw describes. This alone is grist to work with for a character—for example, perhaps they don't realize their condition. But it can be taken further: the scientific name for this condition is prosopagnosia, under which rubric are such difficulties as place recognition, car recognition, or facial expression of emotion. Many funny or dark possibilities spring to mind immediately based on these characteristics. Christopher Nolan's film *Memento* touches on aspects of this condition—in his portrayal of Leonard Shelby, Guy Pearce maintains an expression that is largely unemotional. Has he forgotten himself, his face, his feelings, etc.?

One simple extension of this is to look at people who do what they can to limit or open out to sensory input. Some critics look at Bauhaus architecture and furnishings from this point of view, saying that the lack of ornamentation and the effort to integrate everything in a given structure created something impersonal and bland. Perhaps you or your character has been in someone's home that was completely devoid of art on the walls, or knickknacks, and so on.

In other circumstances, I've noticed people who prefer the other direction, invoking a kind of modern rococo approach by stuffing their living space with as much junk as possible. As we know, there are entire television series about hoarders. Where would your character fall along this blank-wall-to-junk-shop curve? What might they hoard? What kind of stuff might they collect? Would it be collector-type objects such as crystal or rare dolls, or would it be anything green or made in Latvia? If their walls are empty, what lies behind that choice? Do they not see the blankness? As I've urged before, try to suspend judgment. We can't know what lies behind choices unless we talk to people or spend some serious time doing research.

Mental space can fall into this category as well: a lot of us took LSD back in the day, hoping to expand our consciousnesses. Others chose to shut out the world in favor of something more controlled.

---

43. Henshaw, *A Tour of the Senses*, 194.

In both cases, some people fell into cults for either good or ill. What we see may be as much based on our philosophy of living as it is about our eyes. It's hard to understand why anyone would follow a Jim Jones to Guyana and drink the Kool-Aid. We ask: "Couldn't they see what was going on?"

A step in a different direction is to consider how your character interacts with the natural world. Certainly if they are a painter or any other kind of artist who hopes to reflect what they see in the world, we can assume a particular kind of vision on their behalf. Stay open to the possible variations in all cases. When tasked with a still life assignment a friend painted a raw steak bleeding on a counter. Not exactly your bowl of fruit, but a still life nonetheless.

Paul Cézanne said something that I echo in a different way: "I am a consciousness. The landscape thinks itself through me."[44] I often tell my students that if they are working in a very aware fashion, digging deeply into their work, they won't have to think about the characters or plot for long because their script will be thinking about them. Otherwise, why do we suddenly get an idea in the shower when we weren't trying to puzzle out the script?

Another variation on this is to consider what your character finds attractive in another person. There is a moment when one encounters the face and physical reality of another and feels highly compelled toward that person. Whether we think of it as sexual attraction or spiritual connection doesn't matter; something about that person is speaking to us wordlessly. Perhaps they simply resemble a parent in a certain way. Maybe they look like we would like to, as handsome or beautiful as we might wish to be.

By contrast, what happens when we see someone we instantly judge in a pejorative manner? Racism, sexism, ageism, religious extremism, ethnic "cleansing," etc., are all aspects of human behavior that have been around since before history recorded their dreadful results.

The range of what we mean by vision is extremely broad. If you close this book for a moment and look up, what do you see? What do you feel about what you see? What would you rather see?

---

44. Cezanne, Paul. "I Am a Consciousness." Accessed 17 October 2014. http://www.goodreads.com/quotes/100731-i-am-a-consciousness-the-landscape-thinks-itself-through-me.

Or not? What would you like to see before your life is over? What would you like another person to see in order for them to become well or more appreciative or open? What would you prefer the world looked like? Lady Bird Johnson tried to do something about the plethora of advertisement billboards on American highways, with some degree of success.

In many ways, perhaps the ultimate question about vision is this: what would you like to see on screen or on stage? Dig deeply into that question and then write the script that answers your question.

Fade Out

Get out of your writing space! Go to museums and galleries. Take in as much art as you possibly can. Allow yourself to spend time with works that grab your attention. Be sure to seek out a work of art that you don't feel compelled toward and take it in. Ask yourself questions about light and line, subject matter, color: what am I seeing? What was the artist trying to do (as you can best guess)? Pay attention to everything about the space in which the art is displayed. At the Modern Museum of Art in New York and the Hirshhorn gallery on the National Mall in Washington, D.C., there are sculpture gardens to visit, which provide a very intriguing contrast to seeing sculpture indoors. If you're inclined toward history or science, take yourself to those sorts of museums or the kinds one encounters on highways, such as the World's Largest Popcorn Ball, in Sac City, Iowa, or the Cadillac Ranch near Amarillo, Texas.

See performance work you might not normally attend. Maybe you do so only once, though there's a lot to be gained by greater exposure. See modern dance, see ballet, go to the opera, and take in sporting events. If you live in a big city, seek out places where people perform on the street. I used to roam through Central Park or Washington Square Park on Sundays where one could find massive amounts of entertaining things to watch: impromptu music performance, parkour displays and all manner of athletic activities. Simply observing people being out and about can be a great training ground for your writer's eye: ask yourself to take note of what you look at when you first notice a person. What do you tend to look for first? Challenge yourself to really see other people. Do you notice that you tend to glance past certain people or "types" of people?

Engage yourself in other creative modes. Get a digital camera. It doesn't have to be something with all kinds of professional accoutrements; a point-and-shoot will do just fine. Try documenting the places you travel through on a daily basis. See how you like to frame them or look at aspects you know are there but never really spend time observing. Take a painting or pottery class. Maybe what you make is dreadful but you will have an appreciation of the artist's hand and eye from the experience.

You might also gain a lot from simply seeking out places to be away from your normal writing space, such as a park bench or pedestrian bridge. It's hard for us in this technological, hyperactive world to sit still but there are great rewards for doing so. Merely observing the flow of a river or the movement of trees on a windy day, the pattern of vegetation growth or even the way in which traffic moves at a given time can be great stimuli for your eyes.

The key is to watch, know you're watching and let whatever you are seeing really enter your observer consciousness. This is true for all the senses: awareness makes all the difference.

CHAPTER SIX

Visualization
Workshops for Your Senses

"The mind is like a richly woven tapestry in which the colors are distilled from the experience of the senses, and the design drawn from the convolutions of the intellect."
—Carson McCullers, author

As you may have already noted, the preceding chapters focus on writing and exploration. Makes sense: we're working in the scriptwriting world.

There is a lot to be gained, however, from doing explorations that are not focused on writing so much as they are about encouraging direct experiences with your senses. To assist with your sensory awareness, Chapter 6 focuses on visualization etudes that are experiential and not based on writing except as an aftereffect.

In my years of doing improvisational and exploratory work in classes and rehearsals, I've used the first exercise in this chapter the most consistently. It has no formal title other than "All Senses Etude."

A caveat: the All Senses Etude probably falls under the rubric of "touchy-feely," in the sense that it can involve dealing with the evocation of a memory. The memory part can be tricky for some people, in which case I'd strongly encourage you to focus on imaginary circumstances instead. Other etudes throughout the book might evoke personal memories somewhat, though the vast majority are straight-ahead writing etudes. Just keep in mind that the choice of doing a given exercise—and how far you take it—is up to you.

The purpose of the etude is to engage your senses as fully as possible. It can serve you as a prewriting exploration or you may

Visualization

use it in other ways, which I'll explain at the end of the exercise. All you need is a willingness to play and to let go of predicting results.

It is vital that the etude be done with an open mind. We are often too caught up in statistics, deadlines and products to be willing to be process-oriented. The etudes do not come with guarantees. Some will work for you better than others; some may not work at all. It's a matter of discovery and self-awareness. Keep this in mind: be willing to let go of anything that's not working for you—but plan to return on another day, rather than simply quit. Resistance on your part is its own valuable exploration: What stopped me, am I afraid, is this a trigger for something I haven't resolved? Examining reluctance to engage with anything is gold, provided you're able to do so with compassion and fairness. After all, a given sense may not be available to you in one work session, but show up on another occasion; these things come and go.

Even the slightest hint of a given sense is sufficient; maybe you can't smell the entire Thanksgiving dinner but that one whiff of turkey or pie is actually enough to place you in the locale of the memory. Sensory work is not something one can control like a joystick. You must be willing to explore, stay open and avoid being result-driven.

All Senses Etude

Find a place where you can focus without interruption.

Either sit or lay down, and begin to relax. Try not to fall asleep. It's okay to change positions if you need to fight drowsiness, even to stand or take a quick break to dance or jump around to reenergize.

Close your eyes (keep them closed throughout this entire exercise except to check on steps; you can also have someone read the steps to you). Allow your breathing to slow. If you wish, you may do a measured breathing. Find a count that feels right to you, say, a count of six. Inhale for a steady count to six, hold your breath for the same duration and then release steadily for the same count. Take a few minutes to do this in order to slow down your heart rate a bit and take your mind off the events of your day. Do not try to undertake this etude when you're having an emotionally complicated day or if you have an appointment or other time constraint.

Once you feel relaxed, allow yourself to imagine that you are sitting or lying someplace near water and it's a season when the temperature is pleasant enough that you're in a bathing suit, shorts and tee shirt, or any loose, comfortable clothes. "Water" can mean anything from an ocean to a stream to a water sprinkler in a yard. Trust your first choice, which may be a memory or someplace you're simply imagining. It's up to you and your intuition on the day you undertake the exercise.

Once you begin, allow yourself time to explore each sense as fully as you're able. There is no benefit to rushing through.

Step One: Visual. This is the most accessible entry point for most people. Begin by asking: What do I see? This is done by seeing the place within your mind. Take note of scenery, people, structures and anything else that your mind's eye sees. Without physically moving, try to have a 360-degree sense of what is there and be sure to take in yourself as part of this. What you're wearing, the colors you notice around you, the kinds of activities taking place are all observations of equal value. Be diligent in examining the visual world and give yourself plenty of time and space to observe any details you can. Can you see faces clearly? Are there people you know?

The following are critical things to keep in mind: 1) be aware that your mind may decide randomly to blend two or more places together, placing people in a location they were never in or could not experience; 2) it doesn't matter if you don't know the place in which you find yourself—allow your mind to do what it needs; and 3) the environment in which you are doing the exercise may occasionally intrude, so that you notice something in the room rather than in your imagination or recall (an annoying air conditioner hum; the room temperature is colder than the place you are sense-visiting). In every situation, trust what's happening without judgment of it. If you get distracted, allow yourself to return gently to the exercise. If your mind creates a situation that is psychologically or emotionally complex, simply observe it and continue with the exercise. When the session is over, you can analyze it, but in the moment you must be as open as possible to whatever happens. Lastly, you may find that your entry point is through another sense; trust your instincts on this.

Step Two: Auditory. Ask yourself what you can hear in this place by water. Be very broad in your interpretation of this. You may be near a concert, in the middle of a flock of cell phone loud-talkers or in the wilderness. In all your work, a tiny fragment is as good as the whole thing: the softest stirring of leaves by a breeze is equal to a band playing; sound equals sound, period. Try to listen in layers, asking yourself to go deeper and deeper until you've explored all the sounds around you and even within you (is your stomach gurgling?). You may discover that the least audible and subtle sounds are the most interesting and useful.

Step Three: Gustatory. Do the same steps with the sense of taste. What does your mouth taste like on this day, in this place near water? Have you had anything to drink or eat? Are you anticipating having food or drink; can you imagine how it will taste? Keep in mind that you may have a taste in your mouth at the present moment in which you're doing the exercise. You need to acknowledge it and move on to the sense of taste in the place you're imagining or recalling. Be aware that taste can be directly connected to the sense of smell. One can enhance the other.

Step Four: Olfactory. Now try to get a sense of smell. Although some people have difficulty with this, others get an immediate rush of the smells around them. Be willing to dig deeply into this particular sense. You may also want to coach yourself by suggesting odors that might logically be present in this memory. If you're on a beach, do you smell the sea, lake or river? If there are other people around, are they wearing sun block or cologne? Does the area immediately around you have a specific scent, such as wet grass or hot asphalt? Try to get a sense of your own scents—sweat, a freshly laundered tee shirt heating in the sun—anything that is immediately yours.

Step Five: Aspects of Touch. The next sense we will break down into the four elements of touch based on how our bodies experience the world.

The first is tactile, which is the sense of surface. Tactile is our awareness of when something is smooth or rough, and to what degree. If you're wearing a tee shirt or swimsuit or cutoffs in your sense recall, see if you can experience the texture on your skin. Try also to sense the textures of your skin. Our bodies are comprised of extremely varied surfaces we pay little attention to on a daily basis. This is an opportunity to find a greater self-awareness. Remember to focus as well on the surface your body is resting on: towel, chair, grass or sand; try to stay aware of your entire body.

The second element of touch is thermal, the sense of hot or cold. If you are in the sun in your sense recall, try to feel it on your skin and clothes, and measure the difference. If you're in shade, what does that feel like? Have you been perspiring? Is there a temperature difference between places where your clothes or body are wet or dry? You can also imagine moving from sun to shade, or vice versa, or simply shifting position.

Next is kinesthetic, used here to mean the sense of relative tension or relaxation. Are you experiencing a particular emotion in your sense recall? How are your feelings being reflected in your posture, your sense of how your body fits in the remembered space? Are you normally tense, even if feeling happy and positive? How do you relate to your physical self in this regard? As you recall the place you chose, how aware are you now of your musculature? During the exercise was there any kind of physical discomfort that would have been normal for the time you are revisiting? Again, keep in mind these prompts are in relation to the imagined or recalled place in the etude.

When you reach this portion of the exercise, take a few moments to return to your breathing. You can do this throughout the etude. Check to see that your breaths are still coming at a regular rhythm. By this point, you should be in a pretty deep state of relaxation, but it's worth it to do a quick diagnostic. Begin by concentrating on your feet, seeing if there's any tension there, then work your way slowly up your body. You can flex or stretch as you need to, in order to release tension. Remember to return to the place near water and once there reexamine your level of tension. Keep in mind this is a relative matter: you may have been very tense in the imagined place for some reason and it may be affecting you now in the exercise or vice versa.

Finally we come to kinetic, which is the sense of movement through space. This relates directly to your body in motion, and therefore we come to it last. The final phase of the etude requires that you leave your place of rest and jump into the nearby water.

This may mean plunging into a lake or just running through a sprinkler. Regardless, it is the point at which the etude is over; the jump in the water is a way of making a very strong break from where you've been previously. As throughout the exercise, keep this as an imagined effort, rather than actually getting up. Try to be aware of your body in motion as you rise and move to the water,

Visualization 153

then leap in. Experience the relationships between feet and surface, body and air, body and liquid.

Once you've had a chance to experience the water, allow yourself to return to a completely alert state. Open your eyes and take a few moments to observe where you are. Then spend some time reflecting on the exercise. Which parts were enjoyable? Which parts were less enjoyable? Were there any sense aspects that eluded you (keep in mind the value of a whiff or a glimpse)? Were there any sense aspects that overwhelmed you? Did anything surprise you? These are just a few sample questions. No doubt you'll have your own and they will likely change as you repeat the exercise.

It can be valuable to do some writing after the etude is over. I recommend it. You might simply jot down some observations or do some creative work—a scene, a poem—if anything is evoked by the exercise.

This is an etude you can do as often as you wish. It can be done at any point during your day, as a method of regular self-checking, even if only for a minute. We all tend to develop habitual tension places, especially in our work efforts. Writers are prone to sore necks, backs, shoulders, hands and wrists. If you check in from time to time on your state of tension, it's much easier to discover areas that are experiencing degrees of strain and react accordingly. If you take a bit of time to experience the world inside your mind it can relieve interior stress and perhaps even writer's block.

Plan to create your own scenario(s) if what's outlined here becomes too predictable for you. If you wish to relive a specific memory, rather than use this generic approach, keep in mind that memories contain emotions, sometimes very powerful ones; you'll need to be prepared to relive what you choose to recall. Plan to read up on what's known as "affective memory," an exercise devised by the Russian actor and theorist Constantin Stanislavski. Affective memory is also known as "sense memory" and "emotional memory." You will find many intriguing perspectives on the pluses and minuses of this kind of work; it may be best to undertake memory exploration in a class with a qualified acting teacher.

Some additional thoughts about the exercise: first, this kind of work is based on a willingness to touch base with one's emotions and intuition. Intuition means the ability to understand something without the need for conscious reasoning. It is that aspect of us which is often taught out of our child-selves, and with which we writers must reconcile to stay in contact as we make our art.

Intuition is gut feeling. It is "the signal fire flashing on" that an artist must learn to trust. It is the part of us we seek to liberate through experience, which our carefully developed craft techniques will support as we follow our noses into a concept or idea.

It bears repeating that you must undertake this etude, or any other, with an open mind. A critical key to any of the etudes in this book is the willingness to suspend judgment and to let go of any attachment to results. You may find, for instance, that although an etude suggests you go one way, your unpredictable mind takes it somewhere else. Let it. Trust it and be observant so that you have some awareness of where you're going. If you find yourself in a place and don't know how your mind got there, you can try to trace backwards to discover what original thought triggered the departure. This can be a fascinating self-study as you become more aware of the paths your mind tends to take from one thought to another.

Second, as I suggested previously, you may want to do this with a partner. This will help you to stay within your eyes-closed state but could also assist if the partner keeps an eye on your level of relaxation and feeds you each sense one at a time, over a relatively long period. Do not rush this exercise, especially for the first time. Take at least ten minutes from start to finish. By giving yourself leave to ignore time while someone else keeps an eye on it, you can make the experience deeper.

If you don't have a partner, you can record yourself providing the prompts over time. You can use an electronic device to signal the move to the next prompt.

Again, spend some time writing after doing the exercise. It doesn't matter if it's writing on a given project or just random jottings. Nor does it matter if you write about the exercise experience itself. The point is to take advantage of opening your sensory channels by using them for creative and/or reflective work.

Finally, this etude can be done for any type of locale. I have a vivid memory of being at a very high part of the Rocky Mountains, up where the land is tundra and where stepping off a designated path would destroy growth that would take many years to restore. I only need to think of this place and give in to the memory to experience the sharpness of the wind on my face, the clarity of the air, the smell of the nearby snow and so on. All this stuff is there all the time for us, just waiting for us to reexperience it and make use of it for our art.

First Day of School Etude

This is a direct variation on the All Senses Etude.

After establishing a place of relaxation and getting your body open, decide on a first day of school that you remember well. This might be your very first day of school ever or it may just be the first day you can recall, even as late as middle school. Do your best to pick a day that's not fraught with too much tension and craziness so you can work through the senses without bumping into the school bully or worse.

As with the All Sense Etude, begin with what you see and stay loose to the exercise shifting you from one grade or school to another. You may even find yourself out of school and at a camp of some kind. It makes no difference.

Take plenty of time. Visualize the room, the other kids, the teacher. If possible, try to see yourself in a mirror, just to give yourself the opportunity to reexperience your much younger body.

Move through the other senses; give yourself lots of latitude for exploration. Keep an open mind to what you experience. In our current lives we may remember the odors in our elementary school with some distaste, but our six-year-old self might not have noticed them. Suspend judgment as best you can.

Once you've gone through the senses completely, accomplish the very last part by going out of the building and on to the playground. You can stay there for a while or just slowly ease out of the etude once you've successfully arrived at the swing set or wherever you were heading. Take a moment to observe the playground area through your senses and steadily release the sensory recall.

As with the previous etude, you might want to make time to write about your experience in the form of journal notes or give yourself the space to do some creative work.

You can do either of these etudes many times over and vary them as much as you like. You can choose any number of first experiences: first kiss, first graduation day, first time driving on your own, etc. Just be sure to pick something that is vivid to you.

Shapeshifter Etude

This exercise can be useful as a way of concentrating and moving your mind away from the day's stresses. It is also less broad in sensory scope, less time consuming and less apt to bring up old memories.

Once again, begin by relaxing, either sitting or lying down. Close your eyes.

Once reasonably relaxed, focus on seeing a circle. It can be a huge circle, a tiny one, or multitudes of circles. Allow your mind to flow with whatever comes up and don't judge it.

Once you have the circle visible in your mind, make it a blue color. It doesn't matter what shade of blue or if only part of the circle takes on the color. Go with whatever happens, even if you get pink instead—minds are jokers sometimes.

Next, allow the circle to change to a square. Take note of the color. It may have changed completely or just become darker or lighter. Once you have the square (or rectangle, rhomboid, and so on) visualized, change the color to something new and see what happens.

Finally, move to a triangle of any size or type. Again, change the color to something different.

Allow yourself to stay in the relaxed posture for a while longer, eyes still closed, and give the geometric shapes a chance to cycle themselves through your thoughts. When you're ready, open your eyes.

Take a few moments to reflect on the exercise. As with the All Senses Etude, give yourself time to do some writing. Avoid, at all costs, self-criticism. So your circle turned neon yellow, started spinning, and then zoomed off into space? Great; that was today; tomorrow will be different and maybe even weirder!

Variations on this exercise can include visualizing food you like, then taking apart the finished product in your mind and examining the minute parts that made it. For example, if you take a taco with lettuce, tomato, cheese and sauce, you have a single entity made up of many parts. How many parts? Consider what elements are in the taco itself. Visualize, for instance, where the tomatoes grew. Imagine the hands and face of the person who picked that tomato; continue with speculating on how many people handled the tomato in getting it packaged, shipped, placed on the store shelf, etc. When you focus on the taco shell, you must go back to the field in which the corn grew, how it was picked, how it was processed with calcium hydroxide in order to turn it into *masa harina*, then shaped and cooked and so on. There are a great many steps just to make a simple thing to eat, and if you consider the steps involved in eating, digesting and so forth, you'll see that you can visualize things down to their atoms and to the elements that helped them grow.

★ ★ ★

As stated at the outset, the purpose of this chapter is to help you expand your ability to work through your senses. Many writers rely on their senses constantly while working, so this might not be an issue for you. The question arises, however, as to whether you're receptive in all of your sensory areas and to what degree.

Once you've done these visualization etudes, you'll have a better idea of your receptivity. Working on a regular basis on the etudes throughout the book can help improve your awareness and openness. You will find that your writing will reflect this in a variety of ways, as well as your perceptions of the work of other artists.

Fade Out

There are a number of ways in which you can expand your awareness of exploring sensory work in this manner. For example, you might choose guided meditations. These may be from prerecorded material or in a live context such as a yoga class. Another possibility could involve listening to a work of fiction or poetry on a CD and utilizing a random segment as a trigger for visualizing. In writing workshops, improvisation classes or in social interactions you might encounter people providing descriptions of their experiences that you find evocative. Perhaps the most obvious is listening to music of any kind that moves you. Explore what you hear for its sensory evocation, rather than as dance inspiration or emotional expression. The potential for sensory journeying is available to you through unlimited means. Explore at will!

CODA

Final Thoughts

We are the writers. We can bring joy, peace, quiet reflection, self-recognition, liberation, outrage and innumerable other emotions and awarenesses to the lives of countless other people, all from the shapes on a screen or page that we make to tell a story of some kind.

The more well-rounded you are as a human being, the greater the level of compassion and understanding you will bring to your characters. In all the etudes, whether completely silly or very serious, the spirit within is exactly those two qualities. As a friend quoted to me: "Be kinder than necessary; everyone is fighting a hard battle." This echoes a favorite quote from Henry David Thoreau: "Most men lead lives of quiet desperation and go to the grave with the song still in them."

We come into this world as we do, move through it sometimes dull and unaware, and at other times full of life. I have crossed paths with people with remarkable perceptions, often vastly different from my own. My art and process have grown because of these encounters. This is true from the movies and plays I've seen and read, the numerous other arts I've encountered, food I've tried or made, and so on. All these things have enlivened me; my hope with my books and teaching is to do the same for others.

There's a limit to what any author or mentor can provide, so I want to urge you to give yourself a gift, if you don't already do this: read biographies and autobiographies, study the sciences and humanities, eat foods that you don't normally try, take up a hobby, play a sport, step as far outside of the theatre and film worlds as you can. Become a polymath, a life-grabber. If you're truly brave, write what you want to see, rather than what you think will sell. In truth, none of my books have fit the mold of surefire commercial appeal. I'm not writing for that market; I'm sharing what I know

Coda

with writers who will find what I offer to be of value. If you've gotten to this point in the book, you know that I'm talking to you and in many ways you are talking back with me. Keep in mind that however you are responding to the etudes and ideas, it's your sensibilities that are in play, your artistic awareness. The next question beyond that is: where else can I seek insight and encouragement?

I've found great inspiration from the people whose writings are used as sources through this book. Although I don't reference it directly, I greatly admire the work of Oliver Sachs, particularly *The Man Who Mistook His Wife for A Hat*, in which he examines various neurological conditions that had strange and intriguing outcomes. Several of the works I have drawn from are squarely based on Sachs' work, in the same way that Christopher Vogler's *The Writer's Journey* is the child of Joseph Campbell's *The Hero's Journey*. Other works like *Incognito: the Secret Life of the Brain* by David Eagleman, *Deeply into the Bone* by Ron Grimes and *Taking the Quantum Leap* by Fred Alan Wolf have all influenced how I started thinking about working from the senses and expanded from the initial impulse. In addition, I subscribe online to *Brain Pickings Weekly*, *The New York Times* in a daily digest form, *ArtsJournal* and *HowlRound* (a theatre blog), and to the print magazines *Film Comment*, *American Theatre* and *The Dramatist*. Some of these works might grab your attention; some might put you out for a sound night's sleep; I don't read them all cover to cover, in fact. It doesn't matter. Things that will inspire you will somehow pop up if you just keep your channels open. Just keep looking beyond your own art for things that will expand your thinking and consciousness.

This can certainly include yoga and meditation and the like. Join a quilting group or a roller coaster enthusiast club. Seek out people who like to go on ghost hunts. Everything can be your palette as a scriptwriter.

And go the extra mile when you do study your art. Read work and see films by people you don't know. See all of the movies written by a particular screenwriter and read all the plays written by a chosen dramatist. Read *Variety*, a weekly trade magazine focused largely on the business of Hollywood. Join the Dramatists Guild—there's a reasonable student rate—and read the various publications provided online. Watch TV shows like "Dinner for Five" where guests share a meal and talk about the business of film from a personal point of view. Seek out professional playwrights and screenwriters who live in your area to learn from their experiences—if you're a college student, it's likely you can have your department bring guest artists to your campus. View yourself as a permanent apprentice, as in the old days of blacksmiths and shipwrights: expose yourself to every possible means of continuing to learn your trade.

As a longtime professor in various liberal arts universities, my view is unapologetically based on the ideal of the student who is well read, thoughtful, adept at critical thinking and exchange, and expressively capable in a range of writing and speaking forms. From the reading and observing I've done about scriptwriters, this is a description of the best of the best. Our job is actually multifaceted: we must observe, trust our intuition, exercise craft skill and artistic vision when we're writing, market our work and team up effectively with our collaborators when the script is being produced. The more you know about the greater world beyond the page, the better you will be at pitching ideas and working with the concepts of other artists, and the more likely you will be to achieve success.

Ultimately, our most important foundational asset is observer-consciousness: taking in what's there as it presents itself, i.e., making full use of our senses. It is my hope that the etudes and ideas in this book have encouraged you to pay greater attention to the input the world provides on a daily basis, and seek out all you can experience.

★ ★ ★

In my first book, *Playwriting in Process*, I decided to include my contact information. It resulted in people getting in touch with questions about various things and several situations where I was invited to be a guest artist and teach about the way I work. Authors rarely know whether or how they've affected a reader, so any time I hear from someone it's a gift to me; that includes you: michael-wright@utulsa.edu.

WORKS CITED

Ackerman, Diane. *A Natural History of the Senses*. New York: Vintage, 1990.

Cezanne, Paul. "I Am a Consciousness." Accessed 17 October 2014. http://www.goodreads.com/quotes/100731-i-am-a-consciousness-the-landscape-thinks-itself-through-me.

Coppola, Francis Ford, and Mario Puzzo. *The Godfather*. Screenplay. Accessed 17 October 2014. http://www.script-o-rama.com/snazzy/dircut.html.

Eveleth, Rose. "English Speakers Are Bad at Identifying and Describing Smells." *Smithsonian Magazine*. Accessed 4 June 2014. http://www.smithsonianmag.com/smart-news/english-speakers-are-bad-identifying-and-describing-smells-180949519/.

Fornes, Maria Irene. *Maria Irene Fornes: Plays*. Cambridge, MA: PAJ Plays, MIT Press, 2001.

Graber, Cynthia. "Human Nose Tallies More Than a Trillion Scents." *Scientific American*. Accessed 4 June 2014. http://www.scientificamerican.com/podcast/episode/human-nose-tallies-more-than-a-trillion-scents/.

Henshaw, John. *A Tour of the Senses*. Baltimore: Johns Hopkins University Press, 2012.

Hillerman, Tony. Quoted on http://www.quotehd.com/quotes/tony-hillerman-tony-hillerman-an-author-knows-his-landscape-best-he-can-stand.

Horowitz, Alexandra. *On Looking: Eleven Walks with Expert Eyes*. New York: Scribner, 2013.

Horowitz, Seth S. *The Universal Sense: How Hearing Shapes the Mind*. New York: Bloomsbury USA, 2012.

Joseph, Jenny. "Warning." Accessed 12 October 2014. http://www.barbados.org/poetry/wheniam.htm.

Levitin, Daniel J. *This Is Your Brain on Music*. New York: Plume, 2007.

Works Cited

Midler, Bette. "Oh-My-My Lyrics." Accessed 10 June 2014. http://www.metrolyrics.com/friends-oh-my-my-lyrics-bette-midler.html.

Perkins, Moreland. *Sensing the World*. Indianapolis: Hackett, 1983.

Smith, Glenn. "Alzhiemer's Disease." Accessed 12 July 2014. http://www.mayoclinic.org/diseases-conditions/alzheimers-disease/expert-answers/music-and-alzheimers/FAQ-20058173.

U.S. Department of Health and Human Services, National Institute of Health. "Taste Disorders." Accessed 2 July 2014. http://www.nidcd.nih.gov/health/smelltaste/pages/taste.aspx.

Watts, Alan. *The Book: On the Taboo Against Knowing Who You Are*. Accessed 30 May 2014. http://www.beezone.com/alanwatts/taboobook/the_book_chap_1.html.

Weingarten, Hemi. "A Brief History of Food and Nutrition Labeling." Accessed 2 July 2014. http://blog.fooducate.com/2008/10/25/1862-2008-a-brief-history-of-food-and-nutrition-labeling.

Wellescent.com. "Perpheral Neuropathy Is More Than the Loss of Touch." Accessed 15 October 2014 http://wellescent.com/health_blog/peripheral-neuropathy-is-more-than-the-loss-of-touch.

INDEX OF ETUDES

In Alphabetical Order

Note: Each chapter has a primary etude, known as a "Key Etude," which I've noted below. Only etudes that have names are included, not the "Six Degrees" etude spin-offs.

Etude

20/20 Or ? (Key Etude, Chapter Five)   122

All Senses   149
Animal Eyes   138

Body Image, Eating Disorders and Dieting   50

Chain Food   48
Color   126
Color-Blindness   124

Extreme Taste (Key Etude, Chapter Two)   31

Faded Rose, A   22
Familiar Sounds   67
Fine Print, The   41
First Day of School   155
Food Mood   39
Food Service Industry   44

Hands   93
Health   51

Intimate Touch   98

Index Of Etudes

Mighty Nostril, The   16
Mobility   106
Mouth   49
Much Nose   9

No Nose   11
No Taste   35

Pain   107

Restaurant Customer   46
Ritual Meal   37

Shapeshifter   156
Smell Addiction   13
Smell as Memory (Key Etude, Chapter One)   4
Smell as Plot Element   21
Sound Invasion   64
Sound Job   80
Sound Shift   71
Special Vision   135
Speech and Hearing   74
Standing in the Sky   141

Temperature (Key Etude, Chapter Four)   89
Touch as Self   102
Touch Loss/Super Touch   113

What Do They Listen To? (Key Etude, Chapter Three)   58
Why They're Looking   132

PRODUCED WORKS REFERENCED

Note: I indicate the medium a given work appears in originally, or has a specific origin—such as the BBC production of *The Singing Detective* not to be confused with the equally solid, more compacted version—also written by Dennis Potter—directed by Keith Gordon, or the Jean Cocteau version of *Beauty and the Beast* versus the Disney release; with plays in particular it's difficult to find productions or recordings of productions, so indicating those that are available as films provides you with some opportunity to observe the scripts realized.

Films

30 Days of Night, 21
The 40-Year-Old Virgin, 104

All About Eve, 140
All That Jazz, 139
Amadeus, 62
Amélie, 122
American Beauty, 112
Animal House, 31
Apocalypse Now, 17, 110
Arachnophobia, 104
Avatar, 92

Bananas, 28
Batman Begins, 22
Beauty and the Beast (Jean Cocteau), xi
Being There, 143
Big, 34
Big Night, 44
Birdman, xii
Blade Runner, 126

Blow Out, 80
Blue Velvet, 127
Body Heat, 90
Bonnie and Clyde, 104
Boyhood, xii, 103
Brazil, 112
Breaking Away, 107
Bridge on the River Kwai, 92
Broadcast News, 17

Carrie, 137
Chinatown, 99
Chocolat, 29
A Christmas Story, 30
Citizen Kane, 73
Cloudy with a Chance of Meatballs, 31
The Conversation, 80
The Cook, The Thief, His Wife and Her Lover, 28, 34
Crash (David Cronenberg), 110

Crouching Tiger, Hidden Dragon, 88

The Da Vinci Code, 112
Das Boot, 136
The Day of the Locust, 93
Days of Wine and Roses, 35
The Discreet Charm of the Bourgeoisie, 28

Eternal Sunshine of the Spotless Mind, 12

The Fisher King, 80
Frances Ha, 107

Gerald McBoing-Boing: Jolly Frolics, 70
Ghost, 137
Gladiator, 1
The Godfather, 13, 17, 132

Her, 64, 101
The Hunger Games, 29
The Hunt for Red October, 135
The Hustler, 139

I Am Nancy, 105
The Illustrated Man, 104
It's a Wonderful Life, 116

Jaws, 104
Jeremiah Johnson, 101
Julie and Julia, 46
Juno, xii, 13

Kiss of the Spider Woman (also a play), 39

Koyaanisqatsi: Life Out of Balance, 140
Kramer vs. Kramer, 38

Like Water for Chocolate, 29
Little Miss Sunshine, xii, 125
Little Shop of Horrors (also a musical play), 24

Marty (also a TV drama), 101
Memento, xi, 12, 144
Metropolitan, 106
Midnight Cowboy, 101
Midnight in Paris, 131
Miller's Crossing, 76
The Mist, 21
Moon, 101

Napoleon Dynamite, xii, 107
Nell, 70
Network, 111
Night and Fog, 143
Nightcrawler, 126
Nightmare on Elm Street, 105

One Day in the Life of Ivan Denisovitch, 92
The Oxbow Incident, 141

Perfume: The Story of a Murderer, 11
The Piano, 17
Psycho, 137
The Purple Rose of Cairo, 121

Rachel Getting Married, 84, 143
Radio Days, 80
Raging Bull, 93

Produced Works Referenced

The Raid: Redemption, 88
Rebel Without a Cause, 98
Reefer Madness (also a musical play), 104
Repulsion, 137, 138

Salò, or 120 Days of Sodom, 32
Scent of a Woman, 13
Schindler's List, 127
Shakespeare in Love, 68
The Shining, 137
Shoah, 143
Silence of the Lambs, 135, 137
Silver Linings Playbook, 59
Sleeper, 114
Snakes on a Plane, 104
Solaris (Russian and American versions), 101
Some Like It Hot, 123
Splash, 114
Star Wars: A New Hope, 13
Star Wars V: The Empire Strikes Back, 89, 92

A Streetcar Named Desire, 17, 90
Syriana, 109, 135

Talk Radio, 80
Talk to Her, 62
Three Colors Trilogy, 126
Tom Jones, 28
Trainspotting, 75
Twelve Angry Men (also a play and television production), 141
Twilight, 29

When Harry Met Sally, 28
Who Framed Roger Rabbit?, 69
Wild, 88, 109
Wings of Desire, 142
Winter's Bone, 88

The Year of Living Dangerously, 141

Plays

Angels in America (also an HBO film), 18, 99
Arsenic and Old Lace, 18
The Art of Dining, 13, 29
August: Osage County (also a film), 30

The Bacchae, 22, 33, 88
Black Comedy, 135
Blasted, 32, 109
Blithe Spirit (also a film), 137
Bus Stop, 29

Cat on a Hot Tin Roof, 29
Cats, 57
The Clean House, 36
The Conduct of Life, 109
The Curious Incident of the Dog in the Night, 104

Dinner with Friends, 29

Edmond (also a film), 143
The Elephant Man (also a film), 108

Produced Works Referenced

An Enemy of the People, 141
Equus, 104
Evita, 57

Fat Pig, 143
Fool for Love (also a film), 106
Frankie and Johnny in the Clair de Lune (also a film), 44

The Glass Menagerie (also a film), 108
Glengarry Glen Ross (also a film), 141

Hair (also a film), 120
Happy Days, 101
The House of Blue Leaves, 29
How I Learned to Drive, 102

The Iceman Cometh, 29
Idioglossia (also a film, under the title *Nell*), 70

K2, 90
King Lear, 13
Krapp's Last Tape, 101

The Long Christmas Dinner, 29
Long Day's Journey into Night (also a film), 95

Medea, 33
The Miracle Worker (also a film), 88

'night, Mother, 40
Night of the Iguana (also a film), 90

The Odd Couple (also a film and TV series), 43
Oedipus Rex, 13, 126
Our Town, 18

The Pillow Man, 69, 109

Rent, 57
Romeo and Juliet, 13

Savage/Love & Tongues, 70
The Seafarer, 123
The Sport of My Mad Mother, 109
Spring Awakening, 99
Suddenly, Last Summer (also a film), 90
Summer and Smoke (also a film), 90
Sunday in the Park with George (also a film), 127
Sweeney Todd: The Demon Barber of Fleet Street (also a film), 94, 112

The Transfiguration of Benno Blimpie, 34

Wait Until Dark (also a film), 135
Water by the Spoonful, 13
The Water Engine, 80
When You Comin' Back, Red Ryder?, 29
Who's Afraid of Virginia Woolf? (also a film), 76

Produced Works Referenced

Television Shows

"Dinner for Five," 159

"Grey's Anatomy," 91

"L.A. Law," 60

"Listening Is an Act of Love" (PBS animated series), 84

"M★A★S★H," 5

"MasterChef Junior," 45

"Mind of a Chef," 30

"NYPD Blue," 20

"Orange Is the New Black," 16

"The Singing Detective" (BBC production), 37

"The Sopranos," 53

"Top of the Lake," 17

"Treme," 82

"Twin Peaks," ix, xiii

"Weeds," 53

Radio

"Serial," 81

"Snap Judgment," 81

"This American Life," 81

"War of the Worlds" (Orson Welles), 80